60 YEARS
BEHIND THE WHEEL

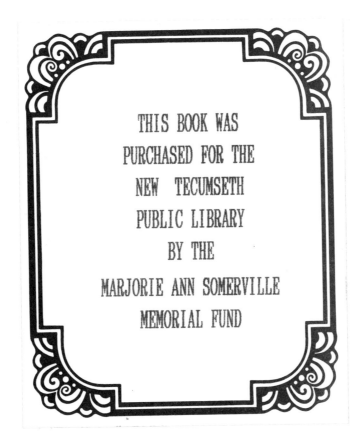

To my loving wife Brenda,
my front-seat passenger on the highway of life,
whose faith and encouragement helped make this book a reality

60 YEARS BEHIND THE WHEEL

The Cars We Drove in Canada 1900–1960

Bill Sherk

A HOUNSLOW BOOK
A MEMBER OF THE DUNDURN GROUP
TORONTO · OXFORD

Publisher: Anthony Hawke
Copy-Editor: Andrea Pruss
Design: Jennifer Scott
Printer: University of Toronto Press

National Library of Canada Cataloguing in Publication Data

Sherk, Bill, 1942-
    60 years behind the wheel : the cars we drove in Canada, 1900-1960 / Bill Sherk.

ISBN 1-55002-465-5

1. Automobiles — Canada — History. I. Title. II. Title: Sixty years behind the wheel.

TL26.S456 2003   388.3'42'0971   C2003-904043-7

    2   3   4   5   07   06   05   04   03

We acknowledge the support of the **Canada Council for the Arts** and the **Ontario Arts Council** for our publishing program. We also acknowledge the financial support of the **Government of Canada** through the **Book Publishing Industry Development Program** and **The Association for the Export of Canadian Books**, and the **Government of Ontario** through the **Ontario Book Publishers Tax Credit** program, and the **Ontario Media Development Corporation's Ontario Book Initiative.**

Printed and bound in Canada.✪
Printed on recycled paper.

www.dundurn.com

Dundurn Press	Dundurn Press	Dundurn Press
8 Market Street	73 Lime Walk	2250 Military Road
Suite 200	Headington, Oxford,	Tonawanda NY
Toronto, Ontario, Canada	England	U.S.A. 14150
M5E 1M6	OX3 7AD	

From rumble seats and running boards to power tops and tailfins, this book captures in stories and photographs the thrill of motoring in Canada from the dawn of the twentieth century to 1960

TABLE OF CONTENTS

FOREWORD
by Mike Filey

WHEN I WAS JUST A young teenager attending North Toronto Collegiate Institute (the finest high school in North America and coincidentally the school at which the author of this book taught, long after I was there), I was never tempted by such mundane propositions as beer, cigarettes, or skipping class. Not me. However, I was often tempted by another, the desire to own a car. In fact, my friend John Ross, who was employed in the family contracting business and really didn't need an education to make his way through life, would just happen to drive by in his new red 1958 Pontiac convertible as I made my way to school along Broadway Avenue. This guy would drive me crazy. He had a nice car, I wanted a nice car. Several times I came close to giving it all up. I'd simply quit school, go out and buy myself something new and flashy, and worry about paying for "my" car in the next life.

Well, that just wasn't to be. First off, I didn't even have my driver's licence. In fact, my parents were adamant that my schooling would come first and if I stuck with it, my dad would teach me to drive and let me use his new, but rather commonplace, 1959 Ford two-door sedan when it came time to take the test. The big day came and I passed. Now it was my turn to get a car. Actually it was a stretch to call what I was able to afford a car at all. It was a 1949 Morris Minor with one option, a heater, the fan of which was under the passenger's seat. Turn the device on and the person sitting beside me would rise two or three inches. The car also had mechan-

ical brakes, a set of flipper directional signals, and was constantly infused with a not totally objectionable (at least not to me) aroma of burning oil. Well, I couldn't do anything about the heater, the brakes, the signals, or that smell, but I could certainly make the vehicle look flashier. I'd give it a do-it-yourself paint job. (Actually, I'd have to do it myself, the fifty bucks I paid for this thing left me flat broke.) So off to the Yonge and Church streets Canadian Tire store I went and bought several tins of paint that when mixed together would give me that turquoise colour I wanted. At least I was pretty sure they would.

As it happened the colour turned out okay, but the amount I had to work with wasn't quite enough. When I reached the trunk area I realized I could never reproduce the colour I had created. What to do? Simple. I went back to the front of the car and pushed the paint towards the back of the car, hoping to move enough along to cover what was left of the original maroon colour.

The old Morris may have been my first car, but it certainly wasn't my last. Far from it. I went through cars like some of my friends went through packs of cigarettes. After the Morris came a 1954 Nash Metropolitan that really wasn't mine. It belonged to Joan Lewis, the wife of druggist Phil Lewis, and as a kind of perk for working in his store at Eglinton and Redpath for an outrageously high number of hours, at an outrageously low hourly rate, I was allowed to use this tiny "babe magnet" on weekends. Next came a

1958 Hillman (never started when it looked like rain) Minx. On this one I spray-painted the hubcaps gold. One day while driving down a country road north of the city one of the caps shot off the car into a farm field. I could only imagine someone finding it years later and believing they had come across remnants of one of those abandoned gold mines out near Markham.

Finally, I graduated (Ryerson, Chemistry, class of 1965 ... actually I took that subject 'cause one of the guys I chummed with had a car and since he was going to Ryerson I decided to join him so I wouldn't have to wait for the bus), got a job, and, of course, bought a brand new car, my first. It was a lovely turquoise and green 1965 Ford Fairlane Sports Coupe. Wow!! One problem, though: I hadn't been working long enough to accumulate a "down payment." Heck, I didn't even know what a "down payment" was. Yarmila, my girl-

friend and later my wife, came to the rescue. Hope she doesn't read this, don't think I ever repaid her.

Now a working stiff, the new cars came fast and furious: 1967 Mustang fastback (should have kept that one), 1967 Dodge Monaco (should never have bothered with that boat), 1968 Mercury Montego (that one almost prevented a wedding — mine), where am I? ... 1970 Ford Torino followed by a 1972 version. Now the cars start to blur, but I remember visions of a Plymouth Arrow (a what?), a 1980 Pontiac Grand Prix, a couple of Toyota Celicas, a Honda Prelude (did I have two of them?), and a couple of Saturns. Oh, I hear you ask, what was the best car I ever owned? The one my wife of many, many years bought for me when I turned fifty-five, my classic 1955 Pontiac Laurentian, just like the one I coveted all those years ago.

INTRODUCTION

FOR OVER ONE HUNDRED YEARS, Canadian motorists have travelled the streets and highways of this vast Dominion in many different makes and shapes of automobiles, many of which are no longer built. Remember the bullet-nose Studebaker? The step-down Hudson? The Nash Metropolitan? How about Hupmobile, LaSalle, Durant, Graham-Paige, Packard, Pierce-Arrow, and DeSoto?

And even with cars still being built, we have names that have passed into history, including Lincoln-Zephyr, McLaughlin-Buick, the "490" Chev, the Model T Ford, the Chrysler Airflow, the Mercury 114, and the Curved Dash Oldsmobile.

All these vehicles at one time were brand new and sparkling clean, fresh from the factory and showroom floor. And nearly all of them were mass-produced on an assembly line, with each one looking much like the one ahead and the one behind.

But every time a new car leaves the factory, it becomes unique and unlike any other car in the world. Each new owner takes it where he or she wants to go, often picking up scratches and dings along the way. The second owner does the same, and the third, and fourth, and so on until the car often reaches its final resting place in a scrapyard.

Each owner gives the car a unique experience, adding another chapter to its "auto-biography." And during the life of that car, someone with a camera is often there to capture the moment. This book contains almost 150 such moments, giving us a glimpse into the past and the way we drove.

Bill Sherk Collection

"Look, Ma! No Steering Wheel!"

THIS CAR IS SO OLD it doesn't even have a steering wheel. Steering is by tiller. It's a Curved Dash Oldsmobile, a popular model in production from 1901 through 1906, and powered by a horizontally mounted one-cylinder engine. Over twenty thousand of these sporty little runabouts were sold. The first one into Canada was reportedly purchased by a minister in Oil Springs, Ontario. The one seen here is participating in a parade of jalopies along Lakeshore Boulevard in Toronto in 1930.

In October 1901, Roy Chapin left the Detroit factory in a Curved Dash Olds, crossed the Detroit River into Windsor, Canada, on a car ferry, and drove across southern Ontario, heading for the second annual auto show in Madison Square Garden in New York. The trip took over seven days, but he made it. When he arrived at the Waldorf-Astoria Hotel, he was so dusty and dirty from driving hundreds of miles on primitive roads that the doorman refused to let him in. He entered through the back door. The publicity generated by this trip was the best advertisement a car company could have, and these little Oldsmobiles began selling as fast as the factory could crank them out. Chapin's route to New York took him across southern Ontario because that was the shortest route. The Canadians who saw him whizzing by at his top speed of 25 miles per hour, or mired in the mud, were probably getting their very first look at this new invention.

Back then, and even today at antique car events, these little Oldsmobiles were easily recognized by their dashboard, which was curved for better visibility. And how did the word "dashboard" come to be applied to the part of a car in front of the driver? The answer can be found in *500 Years of New Words*:

That part of an automobile we still call the dashboard can be traced back to the days of horses and buggies. The Oxford English Dictionary (OED) defines dashboard as "a board or leather apron in the front of a vehicle, to prevent mud from being splashed by the heels of the horses upon the interior of the vehicle." The first writer who used the word (according to the OED) was John Lang in "Wanderings in India," published in 1859: "He fell asleep, his feet over the dashboard, and his head resting on my shoulder."[1]

Webster's Ninth New Collegiate Dictionary dates the word even farther back — to 1846.

Modern-day auto buffs who pride themselves on precision in language prefer to call the dashboard the instrument panel because it's no longer there to protect you from chunks of mud flying from horses' hooves.

Winton Runabout, Toronto, circa 1904

THIS AMERICAN-BUILT, RIGHT-HAND-drive Winton attracted a crowd of mostly men and boys in front of the King Edward Hotel in downtown Toronto in the early days of motoring. The hotel was named in honour of Edward VII, the reigning monarch (1901–1910) and an early enthusiast of motor cars.

The "King Eddy" first opened its doors in 1903, and on July 27 of that year, it provided the venue for the first general meeting of the Toronto Automobile Club, which had already set up a perma-

nent office in the hotel. Through amalgamation with similar clubs in Hamilton, Ottawa, and Kingston, the Ontario Motor League was born in 1907.

The Winton was named for Alexander Winton, who began building automobiles in Ohio in 1897. One of his first customers was John Moodie of Hamilton, who imported a Winton into Canada in 1898. The one shown here is typical of cars of that era — no windshield, no doors, and no top. Motorists often bathed or showered after every drive on the mostly unpaved, dusty roads. Note the heavily clothed female passenger and the goggles on the driver's cap.

The headlights shown here are covered, perhaps to protect them from stones flying up from horses' hooves. Even if you intended to drive your car only during daylight hours, you were well advised to equip your car with a pair of headlights. The roads were littered with horseshoe nails, and changing a flat tire could delay your return home until after dark.

Not everyone who owned a Winton was happy with it. One of Mr. Winton's first customers didn't like the car and told him so. To which Winton allegedly replied, "If you're so smart, maybe you should build your own car, Mr. Packard."

James Ward Packard did exactly that, and test-drove his first car in November 1899. Winton automobiles remained in production until 1924. The Packard nameplate survived until 1958.

Cadillac Truck, Toronto, circa 1906

IF YOU WANTED SOME FRESH fruit or game delivered to your house in Toronto around 1906, you picked up your phone (if you had one) and asked the operator for Main 7497 or 7498. The driver at Gallagher & Co. Ltd. crank-started the Cadillac delivery truck from the side and drove off to your address, powered by the ten-horse-power, single-cylinder engine mounted under the front seat. This particular vehicle was perhaps a car converted into a truck, a common practice back then.

Note the folded top behind the driver. This truck no doubt made deliveries in all kinds of weather, and a top would be deemed a necessity. The Cadillac nameplate is visible below the phone numbers, and the hole for the crank is below that. When these noisy engines fired up, nearby horses often reared up in fright.

The Cadillac was named after the French explorer who founded Detroit in 1701, and the car quickly earned a reputation for precision engineering, beginning with its very first model completed in October of 1902. Six years later, eight single-cylinder Cadillacs were shipped to England. Three were selected at random, driven twenty-three miles to the new Brooklands Motordrome, and then completely disassembled. The 721 parts of each were scrambled with the others, and 89 parts were replaced with off-the-shelf substitutes. Cadillac mechanics reassembled the three cars from the 2,163 parts, then drove them at top speed for 500 miles, earning for Cadillac the highly coveted Dewar Trophy for excellence in standardized interchangeable parts.

Breakdown Near Sarnia, circa 1908

SCENES LIKE THIS INSPIRED THE lyrics of a song: "Get Out and Get Under." The car is a Rambler Type One Surrey with a two-cylinder, eighteen-horsepower engine, a model in production from 1904 to 1908. The secondary "steering wheel" operated the throttle. Note the absence of a top or a windshield (usually available at extra cost).

The license number (2994) is clearly visible but with no year of issue. Ontario introduced license plates in 1903 as a convenient new source of revenue, but did not issue annual plates with the year displayed until 1911.

The Rambler was renamed the Jeffery in 1914, after the founder of the company, Thomas B. Jeffery. The Jeffery was renamed the Nash in 1917 when Charlie Nash took over. The Rambler name was revived in 1950 with the introduction of America's first commercially successful post-war compact car, the Nash Rambler.

Jack Greswell, *Leamington Post*

Engineless Car, Leamington, circa 1908

BILLY COLEMAN, OTIS DELAURIER, AND Richard Malott were photographed sitting in this car of unknown make and year with the engine out. Perhaps it's parked outside a shop that rebuilds engines while you wait. The tires are white because that's the natural colour of rubber. Black tires appeared around 1916, when carbon was added to the tires for greater strength.

When this photo was taken around 1908, the Ontario government had been licensing automobiles for five years — and with the steady increase in car ownership, the flow of money into provincial coffers was increasing too. Maybe local county governments could also get a slice of the action.

The following item, entitled "Would Regulate Auto Traffic," appeared in the *Leamington Post* on December 17, 1908:

The Essex County Council has adopted a resolution asking the Ontario legislature for an act permitting each county to regulate and license automobile traffic through its territory.

The action is directed particularly against automobiles from outside the province passing through Essex county, and especially those touring from Detroit, many of which have made nuisances of themselves in every way.

As first introduced by Warden O'Neil, the resolution asked authority to charge a license fee of $25 on each automobile passing through the county. It was pointed out that if adopted in each county, say between Detroit and Niagara rivers, this would make touring prohibitive, and the cost between Detroit and Buffalo would be about $300 in license fees. The resolution was finally adopted without naming a specific amount.

Unfortunately, that news item doesn't explain how Detroit motorists "have made nuisances of themselves in every way." But it's easy to speculate. Some motorists bypassed their muffler with an exhaust cut-out for greater acceleration and top speed, with a deafening increase in noise. And that noise was sometimes loud enough to frighten a horse into bolting — even if the horse was pulling a carriage.

Born to Sell Newspapers, circa 1909

A TORONTO DAILY NEWSPAPER, THE *Telegram*, was founded in 1876 by John Ross Robertson (1841–1918), photographed here standing in the front seat of his chauffeur-driven touring car around 1909. The family is in the back, the luggage is strapped on behind, and the car is ready to go. Robertson himself went many places during his newspaper career, including an 1869 visit to Fort Garry (in what soon became Manitoba), where he was arrested and held for a week by none other than Louis Riel. Robertson devoted his long life to the betterment of Toronto, and he wrote and published the Landmarks of Toronto series, which is still used as the standard reference work on the city's early buildings and people. During his lifetime he gave away large sums of money to worthy causes, and near his death he remarked, "I will surprise everyone by the small amount of money I will leave." He passed away on May 31, 1918, at his home at 291 Sherbourne Street.

In the early 1920s a public school was built at the northeast corner of Glengrove and Rosewell in North Toronto and named in his honour. His newspaper lived on until 1971, when it finally went under. A new paper arose phoenix-like from the ashes of the old: the *Toronto Sun*. What became of Robertson's large and luxurious touring car is unknown.

Fred Foster's 1908 McLaughlin

FRED FOSTER OF BOWMANVILLE, ONTARIO, is seated behind the wheel of his new 1908 McLaughlin Model F two-cylinder touring. Sam McLaughlin began building automobiles in Oshawa, Ontario, in December 1907 with Buick engines imported from the United States and bodies built by McLaughlin. Fred is seen here with his family ready to leave for Midland, Ontario, to attend a family wedding. He was so pleased with his new car he wrote the following letter to the factory that built it:

Bowmanville, December 14th, 1908
Messrs. McLaughlin Motor Car Co. Ltd.
Oshawa, Ont.

Dear Sirs:
The Touring Car I purchased from you last spring has given me the very best of satisfaction. It is economical in consumption of gasoline, and will

climb any hill I have yet met. My repairs for the entire season have cost $2.00.

When I purchased the car I had no knowledge whatsoever of Automobiles. After a few days experimenting I took my family for a trip covering 300 miles, without a chauffeur, and we had no mishap or trouble. During the season I have travelled over 3500 miles, and the car is practically as good as when it left the factory.

I thank you heartily for the great courtesy you and your employees have shown me, and conscientiously recommend the McLaughlin car to anyone desiring a reliable and commodious machine.

Yours truly,

Fred Foster

The little girl seated in the back grew up and became a doctor. Her married name was Ruby Tremer, and she passed away at the end of a long and eventful life. Noel Hamer of Odessa, Ontario, purchased this photo and papers from her husband after she died.

Noel has been restoring antique cars for over forty years. His favourite is the 1932 Ford roadster. He has restored twenty-seven of them.

WHY NOT OWN AN AUTOMOBILE?

If automobiles are needed anywhere at all they are in the country. One of the speakers of the Women's Institute, at Guelph, recently predicted that the time was near at hand when farmer's wives would run their own automobiles. Nor is the prediction a visionary one. Like the telephone and the trolley, the automobile seems destined to add to the comfort of country life, and the cost will not interfere with your buying. We can sell

Good Second-Hand Machines

at a mere fraction of original cost. These cars are taken by us as part payment for the newest and latest models, and are such as we can thoroughly recommend. Any machine we send out is guaranteed to be in first-class condition, and beyond the fact that second-hand cars are not this year's style, there is nothing wrong with them in any way. We use them as a means of introduction to the country trade, and make the values extra special to encourage quick buying. If interested, send your name and address for fuller particulars.

HYSLOP BROS., Limited

High-Class Automobiles and Bicycles   TORONTO, ONT.

"Why Not Own an Automobile?" 1909

IT'S INTERESTING TO NOTE THAT this ad from Hyslop Bros. in Toronto appeared on Thursday, March 18, 1909, in the local newspaper, the *Leamington Post*, in Leamington, Ontario, a community over two hundred miles from Toronto. The ad likely ran in papers all over Ontario and reflected the aggressive marketing policy of this enterprising dealership.

Instant Grandstand, Weston, 1910

WHAT WERE THESE PEOPLE WATCHING from their car parked in a farmer's field in Weston, Ontario, in July 1910? It was the first airplane flight over Toronto. The pilot was French Count Jacques de Lesseps. Grounded by bad weather, Jacques's monoplane, La Scarabee, finally lifted off into clearing skies from the rain-soaked field around 8:00 p.m. and flew at 2500 feet over the Exhibition grounds, then over downtown Toronto, at a speed of 70 miles per hour. Mike Filey of the *Toronto Sun* describes the city's reaction: "Bewildered citizens filled the streets and sidewalks, lined porches and roof tops as they gazed skyward for a glimpse of the first airplane to fly over their city. Torontonians were thunderstruck."

And what about the car itself, serving as a mobile grandstand? It was right-hand drive, and judging by the cap on the head of the driver, it was chauffeur-driven. Chauffeurs back then had to know how to repair cars as well as drive them, since flat tires and mechanical breakdowns were an everyday occurrence. The tool box on the running board was an absolute necessity. The number on the licence plate also appears on the cowl lamps, as required by law — probably to aid the police when the licence plate was too muddy to read. Introduced in 1908 with a price tag of $4,500, this car is a very luxurious Canadian-built Russell Model K "seven-seated" tourer with a fifty-horsepower, four-cylinder engine.

More Cars than Horses, Toronto, 1910

THIS PHOTO WAS TAKEN AT Bay and Adelaide, in front of the Farmers Bank of Canada, which was suspended on Monday, December 19, 1910. Already it was apparent that automobiles were beginning to outnumber horses, at least in downtown Toronto. But traffic was still light, enabling the chauffeur and limousine to park in the middle of the intersection. Judging by the awnings and clothing, the photo was taken in mild weather.

Just ten years earlier, the horse had greatly outnumbered cars in Canada. In the year 1900, cars were so rare that people had not yet decided what to call the new contraptions. Horseless carriage, gas buggy, and motorcycle were some of the early attempts to label this new invention.

Two-car Garage, Leamington, 1912

THE TWO-CAR FAMILY BECAME widely popular in the 1950s, thanks to the rising tide of prosperity that followed the end of the Second World War. Back in 1911, William T. Gregory built a two-car garage that still stands at 43 Mill Street West in Leamington, Ontario. The building to the right was his office, used until recently by his nephew, the late Herbert T. Gregory.

In an interview shortly before his death, Herb Gregory recalled his family owning an Autocar (not the car in the photo), which was garaged in this building. It was tan in colour and built by the Autocar Company of Ardmore, Pennsylvania. Inside the garage was a large green container of bulk oil with a crank to pump it out. "I used to love turning that crank as a boy," he said.

Another make of car Herb recalled was the Hupmobile. His dad and uncle prospered as agents of the Imperial Tobacco Company, with an office in Leamington. The company purchased a fleet of four or five Hupmobile roadsters around 1911 for their tobacco agents to visit farmers. Herb said, "They were little two-seater cars with chain drive and a canvas top. I remember them well."

The large touring car parked in front of William T. Gregory's garage is difficult to identify because of the angle of the photo.

Glenn Baechler, co-author of *Cars of Canada*, reports, " I really exhausted all the candles on this one as it really is a great picture. [The car] has all the features of a Buick but from this view it appears like a longer wheel base. I think it is either a Westcott or a Kissel."

Although the car carries a 1912 Ontario plate, it can't be a 1912 Cadillac. That's the year Cadillac introduced its legendary electric starter, along with electric headlights and cowl lights. The car in the photo has the more primitive acetylene lights.

The car has right-hand-drive, as did most early cars, so the driver could keep a close eye on the ditch while struggling to keep the vehicle on the road. The absence of a rear bumper was the norm in 1912, although many makes offered them as an option. The tool box on the running board was a vital necessity. The spare tire (sometimes two) is presumably mounted on the far side of this car. The identity of the two men is unknown.

The front wheels have ten wooden spokes, while the rear wheels have twelve, no doubt a reflection of the muddy roads and rear-wheel-drive. The extra strain of ploughing through the mud is better spread across twelve spokes than ten.

As a car aged, the wooden spokes would dry out and shrink, causing the wheels to wobble. You then parked your car up to the hubs in a nearby river. The dry spokes would swell up and tighten the wheels, making them as good as new.

Motorcycles and Sidecars, Toronto, circa 1912

BEFORE THE ADVENT OF HENRY Ford's assembly line in 1913 and the start of high-volume mass production, cars for most people were expensive and unaffordable. Hence the early popularity of motorcycles (Harley-Davidson dates back to 1903). Cheaper to buy, cheaper to operate, easy to store — and if you wanted passengers, you could add a wicker sidecar like the two shown here in front of a Tamblyn's Drug Store, circa 1912.

Jack Greswell, *Leamington Post*

New Model T Touring, 1912

LEWIS JEFFREY AND HIS WIFE are sitting in this new 1912 Model T touring near the Albuna Town Line and 5th Concession a few miles north of Leamington, Ontario. It's the last year for the fully vertical two-piece windshield and the first year a Model T was available with front doors. American-built Ts had a false door on the driver's side to reduce the cost of the car. Canadian-built Model Ts had two fully opening front doors because many Ts built here were sold in other provinces and parts of the British Empire where they drove on the other side of the road. British Columbia did not switch from driving on the left until 1923. The Ts sold in these areas had the steering wheel on the right.

Henry Ford pioneered the idea of the steering wheel on the left with the first Model T built in October 1908, at a time when most cars had the wheel on the right. Henry apparently had decided the driver needed to watch the oncoming traffic more closely than the ditch — and this viewpoint was consistent with his goal of building a car that nearly everyone could afford. During its nineteen-year production run, over fifteen million Ts were built. A Ford historian has estimated that 2 percent of these have survived. And 2 percent of 15,000,000 is a staggering 300,000!

1912 Model T Touring, Leamington, 1939

TWENTY-SEVEN YEARS (AND SEVEN miles) separate this photo from the previous one. Note the white-on-black 1939 Ontario plate mounted not in front of the rad but just ahead of the windshield, perhaps for better cooling.

Two names are hand-written on the back of the original photo: "Harry Hartford now dead, Ray Serviss now dead." The author has been able to identify all five occupants, thanks to Jack Hartford and his younger brother Harry Hartford. Their dad, Harry Hartford, is behind the wheel. The front-seat passenger is Jack Robertson. Seated in the left rear of the car is Harry Page. In the centre is Gord Stockwell. Seated in the right rear and wearing a cap is Ray Serviss. It is believed that the car did not belong to Harry Hartford but was lent to him to drive in a parade through town for the Old Boys' Reunion of 1939. Harry owned a Penny Farthing bicycle back then, and "Cider" Hillman may have ridden Harry's bicycle in that same parade.

Harry Hartford operated a Red Indian Service Station on the northeast corner of Talbot and Victoria in Leamington in the 1930s and 1940s (on the original site of Leamington Auto Wreckers dating back to the 1920s). By the 1950s, Harry's station was a Texaco and was operated by his son Jack Hartford.

Is this the same car as the T in the 1912 photo? It's possible, given the same area, but unlikely in light of the high number of Model Ts built and sold. Dick Forster was the first Ford dealer in Leamington, followed by Stodgell and Symes, then Campbell Motors until 1942, then Eaton Motors (1942–54), then Jackson Motors. The current dealer (Land Ford-Lincoln) is preparing to vacate its Talbot Street East property (a former Studebaker dealership) for larger premises on the Highway 3 bypass north of town.

If we look closely at the Model T in the 1939 photo, we can see signs of its age. The headlight lens on the passenger side is cracked, some rad fins are bent, and the top is missing. And yet the car appears still in good shape after nearly three decades on the road (some Ts still driven by then were held together with baling wire). The stickers on both windshields are likely souvenirs of trips to other places.

The three fellows seated in the back appear to have sufficient leg room. When Henry Ford was designing the Model T, he reportedly said the distance between the back of the front seat and the front of the back seat had to be wide enough for a farmer's two milk cans. To keep the cost down, most Model Ts had no fuel pump, no oil pump, and no water pump. When questioned about the lack of shock absorbers, Ford reportedly said, "The passengers are the shock absorbers."

Judy Sherk

Russell Torpedo, Toronto, circa 1911

THIS IS THE FIRST CAR that the late Marjorie Morton of Toronto could remember riding in. Her future brother-in-law's father, Roy Deitch, is standing in front of the car. He was a university student at the time and was hired as a chauffeur for the family that owned the car. The photo was taken "around 1911" on Roxborough Avenue at Chestnut Park in midtown Toronto. The houses in the background are still there, now with many beautiful shade trees. Marjorie (born in 1901) could not remember the name of the car when interviewed by the author in 1995.

The identity of the car was supplied by Glenn Baechler (co-author of *Cars of Canada*):

The car in the picture is a 1912 Russell model '22' Torpedo, built in West Toronto by the Russell Motor Car Co., Ltd., and with a price tag of $3100.00.

A close examination of the picture shows the passengers are wearing hats and overcoats and there are no buds or leaves on the trees, suggesting a late fall scene in 1911. A possible caption …

"Local man takes delivery of the first of the new 1912 Russell models."

Russell created a distinctive angular design for this model and the styling was considered very modern and racy, easily earning the title of Torpedo. The beauty of the stylist was further enhanced with wire wheels. This option was only shown on the model 22 in the 1912 catalogue.

Russell offered four basic chassis in 1912. The Russell 30 was a 4 cylinder regular valve engine while the sleeve valve Knight powered cars came in three sizes. The '38' for its 38 horsepower, the 26 a mid-size model, and the model 22, our subject car with 22.4 horsepower.

The enclosed artists' sketch of the model 22, four passenger touring is from the 1912 Russell catalogue and gives us a view of the other side of the car.[2]

The first Russell cars were known as the Model A. They were launched in 1905 and featured a flywheel with built-in fan blades and a gearshift lever on the steering column (which did not appear on most other cars till the late 1930s). The cars got bigger as time passed, and by 1912 the Russell was firmly established as Canada's leading luxury car.

Unfortunately, production problems plagued two new models introduced in 1913. The following year, war broke out in Europe and the company began the switch to armaments. Then John North Willys of Toledo, Ohio, began building Willys-Overland cars in the Russell factory in West Toronto, and production of this fine Canadian car came to an end. How fortunate we are that someone took the time to snap a photo of the Russell Torpedo we see here.

Glenn Baechler

Car and Trailer, Leamington, 1913

THIS POPE-TRIBUNE MODEL X runabout was photographed in 1913 in front of H.O. Daykin Insurance at 6 Erie Street South in Leamington, Ontario. William F. Sanford is at the wheel, with Jeff Foster beside him. The Deming Hotel in the background was replaced in 1922 by the Bank of Montreal, which still occupies that site today. The Pope-Tribune was manufactured by Colonel Pope in Toledo, Ohio, from 1904 to 1907, making the car in the photo at least six years old. It may have been shipped new by freighter across Lake Erie to the Leamington dock.

The year this photo was taken (1913) was also the first year Canadian motorists were able to join a national organization pro-

moting the interests of the motoring public. The birth of the CAA is superbly chronicled in *Cars of Canada*:

> At the second meeting of the old Toronto Automobile Club, Secretary T.A. Russell had read a letter from the Automobile Association of America inviting the Torontonians to become a division of the AAA. A lengthy debate followed, but finally on the urging of Dr. Doolittle, the idea was rejected. The Americans would be told that while co-operation was a constant goal,

Canadian motorists wanted their own national organization.

This dream came true in 1913, with formation of the Canadian Automobile Association, to which almost all present-day clubs are affiliated. A preliminary meeting on September 3 that year met with such enthusiasm that when a perma-nent organization was set up on December 30 there were 22 clubs from Halifax to Vancouver involved ... Permanent headquarters were set up in Ottawa in 1914.[3]

The town of Leamington began paving its streets that same year.

Cadillac with Horses and Chickens

ONE OF THE OLDEST CARS in Ron Metcalfe's family album is this 1911 Cadillac Model Thirty Torpedo Touring photographed sometime before 1921 at the family farm in Weston (now part of Toronto).

The car was owned by Ron's mother's uncle, Bill Ashbee, and Ron's mother (Dora Banner) is the young girl sitting next to Marion Ashbee, who is behind the wheel. Uncle Bill (standing with the horse) nicknamed his car the "Shadowlet" (rhymes with Chevrolet), perhaps because his Cadillac was big enough to overshadow any Chevy. Bill's leather rear seat can be seen in the left of the photo, suggesting that the Ashbee Cadillac served as a part-time truck.

Before Traffic Lights, circa 1914

FOR MANY YEARS, TORONTO POLICE officers regulated the flow of traffic at major intersections by using a hand-turned "STOP-GO" semaphore like the one shown here at King and Yonge around 1914. They were rolled out (the base was circular) into the inter-sections at rush hour. These officers were in constant danger of being run over, and they no doubt welcomed the arrival of Toronto's first electric traffic lights at Bloor and Yonge on Saturday, August 8, 1925.

Ian Marr

McLaughlin Touring, Charlottetown, circa 1914

IAN MARR OF BAYFIELD, ONTARIO, wrote:

Photo is of my mother, Grace Marr (nee Messervy) taken about 1914 at Charlottetown, P.E.I. at the wheel of my grandfather's 1912 McLaughlin-Buick Touring car. Note the size of the spare tire, coal oil cowl lamps, windshield braces and right hand drive. Buick went to left hand drive in 1914. As an interesting aside, Walter Lorenzo Marr, David Buick's first chief engineer and a co-inventor of the overhead-valve engine, is a distant relative of mine. Also in the car are my grandmother, Carrie Messervy, cousin

Edna Gordon (both in back seat) and Uncle Robert Messervy (with cap in front seat). The others are family friends. Mother survived to age 91 and passed away in 1987 at Kitchener, Ontario. She always thought P.E.I. to be the most beautiful place in Canada with its red soil, green trees, and blue-green ocean and she always referred to it as "The Island!" Her father, J.A. Messervy, the owner of the car, was an M.P. for Charlottetown and her great uncle, George Coles, was a Premier of P.E.I. in the 1850's and a Father of Confederation.[4]

The first gasoline-powered automobile appeared on the Island in 1904 (although Father G.A. Belcourt had driven his steam vehicle there thirty-eight years earlier). But farmers and other rural folk disliked these new contraptions, and Prince Edward Island banned automobiles beginning in 1909, even though there were only nine automobiles on the Island at that time. Finally, in 1913, the ban was lifted.

The McLaughlin Touring owned by Ian Marr's grandfather would have been built at the McLaughlin factory in Oshawa. Sam McLaughlin began building cars bearing his name in 1908 with components purchased from Buick in the United States. In 1918, General Motors of Canada was formed with Sam McLaughlin as president. He led an active life and passed away at age one hundred in 1972.

Ian Marr

Ian Marr's Rockne Convertible, 1944

MARR RECALLED:

This photo taken in the fall of 1944, shows me sitting proudly behind the wheel of my first car, a 1932 Rockne convertible coupe. This car was built by Studebaker only during 1932 and 1933. It was named after Knute Rockne, the famous Notre Dame football coach. The Rockne had a rumble seat and the upholstery was green and yellow leather — pretty snazzy! Beside the Rockne is another rare car — my father's 1942 Pontiac sedan.

Grandfather's Centre-door T, 1926

IAN MARR WROTE: "THIS PHOTO, taken in 1926 shows me at the age of 1 1/2 years with my grandfather's Model T centre door Ford. Note the chains on the rear wheels. This was the start of my love affair with antique cars."

The centre-door Model T first appeared in 1915 and remained in production until the end of the 1921 model year. It was designed to equalize the ease of entry into the front and rear seats, but was an awkward compromise at best. The conventional two-door T sedan gave easy access to the front seat, and the four-door T easy access to front and rear. Both these body styles were introduced in 1923, the same year that nearly two million Model T Fords of all body styles were built.

City of Toronto Achives, Series 372, sub-series 72, Item 403

Toronto Water Works Trucks, 1914

YOU HAD TO BE TOUGH to drive a truck some ninety years ago. Many trucks, like the ones here in St. Andrew's yard on Tuesday, November 17, 1914, had no doors, even if they were driven year-round. And the ones with solid rubber tires could shake your teeth out. They were usually geared low for hauling capacity and didn't have much of a top speed. Ron Fawcett recalled a Model T tanker truck he drove years ago: "It had two forward speeds — slow and slower."

Car Loses Wheel, circa 1914

HARRY MITCHELL OF WALLACEBURG, ONTARIO, no doubt enjoyed seeing his name on the radiator badge of his Mitchell touring, but he did not manufacture it. Mitchell automobiles were introduced by a long-established carriage builder in Racine, Wisconsin, in 1903 and remained in production until 1923, when Nash bought the factory. Like many early cars, Harry's Mitchell was right-hand-drive so he could keep an eye on the ditch. It didn't save him from the mishap seen here.

Licensed As a Car, 1914

A CROSS BETWEEN A MOTORCYCLE AND a car was the so-called "cycle-car." Reverend J.D. Morrow of Toronto owned this one, and swore to wear no hat till his Queen Street West church at Gore Vale had a roof on it. The church finally got its roof, and here is the Reverend Mr. Morrow finally wearing a hat. Note the chain drive. Some of these cycle-cars had a V-2 engine with the steering column through the V. A cycle-car known as the Imp was built in Toronto in 1913.

City of Toronto Archives, Fonds 1244, Item 917

On His Majesty's Service, circa 1915

THIS BRASS-RAD MODEL T Ford served as a commissary wagon for the 83rd Battalion with Major Wilson and Captain Barker around 1915. Although Henry Ford's favourite colour for the Model T was black, this T was an exception. The year 1915 was automotively significant in Canada for two reasons: Tommy Russell of Toronto stopped building cars bearing his name, and William Gray of Chatham, Ontario, began his ten-year run of building Gray-Dorts.

Canadians Celebrate Armistice Day, 1918

THIS TRUCK WITH SOLID RUBBER tires rolled through Toronto as people celebrated the end of the Great War (as it was called until the outbreak of the Second World War). The conflict officially ended at the eleventh hour of the eleventh day of the eleventh month of 1918. Canadians now turned their attention to a future that held the promise of peace and prosperity.

Following a brief post-war depression, automobile production skyrocketed during the 1920s on a wave of prosperity unimagined by previous generations. By 1929, nearly everyone in Canada who wanted a car could buy one, even if it meant shelling out a dollar or two for an old jalopy that still ran.

In 1919, 90 percent of all cars produced in North America were open cars with a folding top and side curtains. By 1929, 90 percent of all new cars built in North America were closed cars. Motorists were demanding — and getting — cars that protected them and their families from the weather. This protection was especially important in Canada, where long, cold winters forced many motorists to put their cars up on blocks until the spring.

By the mid-1920s, motoring had become a national pastime, whether it was a Sunday afternoon drive or a motor trip of several hundred miles. Good paved roads and "filling stations" (as they were called back then) catered to the motorists' growing demand for more roads, better roads, wider roads — and more powerful cars to reach their destination in half the time.

Hauling Telephone Poles, British Columbia, circa 1920

ED BROWN STARTED ONE OF the first trucking businesses in Burnaby, British Columbia, perhaps as early as 1910. His grandson, Jim Ervin, wrote:

> The business was located at the family home at 3131 Royal Oak Ave. in South Burnaby. That was close to the top of one of the steepest hills in Burnaby and must have made for a real test of man and machine to drive it, especially in winter. The children loved it for sleigh riding but probably not their father.

Most of the area was forest at that time and one of Ed's first jobs was to haul shingle bolts out of the forest with a team of horses. My mother used to have to grease the skids placed on the logging trails for the loaded sleds to be pulled out on. One time, as she told me, there was a huge forest fire and my grandfather barely escaped with his life and one last load.

Later, when the area had been cleared, he helped to build the Oakalla Prison Farm, now replaced by townhouses on Royal Oak Ave. This job led to him becoming the first contractor to haul the license plates made by the prisoners. Some of these plates would be worn by Ed's own trucks.

His trucks included some pretty obscure makes such as Hufman, Garford, Stewart (which my mother often said was no good), Gotfredson and the more common names of Chevrolet and GMC. A Ford Model T would probably have been too light for the kind of hauling Ed was doing in the 1920s.

I always thought his main cargo was coal and coke, but I received quite a surprise with some recently discovered information. It started when I was removing boxes of general junk from the house to the garage to make more space. One of those boxes broke open and one item which came out wasn't junk by any means. It was a copy of a business card for Brown's Transfer, a company which hauled coal, coke, wood and did furniture moving as well. My mother often described my grandfather as a "go-getter" for business. I believe I see what she meant. Never was I so glad to have a cardboard box break open and to retrieve such an important item.

People such as my grandfather made a great contribution to Burnaby.[5]

Jim Ervin

JIM ERVIN CONTINUED: "MY GRANDFATHER's business card was rather colourful with an orange border and oval logo. The lettering and cartoons are dark blue. On the back of the card was an ink blotter. Note the price of coal at $10.50 per ton."

Press and Movie Photogs, 1919

THESE EAGER PAPARAZZI HAD THEIR photo taken at Queen's Park, Toronto, in 1919. The Ontario Legislature is just behind them. And the car they are sitting in is easy to identify. The "bow tie" logo on the radiator tells us it's a Chevrolet.

Louis Chevrolet was a race car driver who gave his name to the car that's been the mainstay of General Motors almost from the beginning. Flamboyant and high-spending Billy Durant was the irrepressible entrepreneur who formed GM in 1908 by bringing several car companies together. He decided the future of the auto industry lay in consolidation — and he was right.

But disagreements with the other directors led to his being ousted from the company. Determined to regain control, he started a new car company in 1911 to provide the leverage he needed to regain control of GM. The car was Chevrolet, and it put him back in power till he was ousted a second time — this time for good.

Meanwhile, GM introduced the "490" Chev in 1915 (named for its advertised list price) to compete against Henry Ford's Model T. Some of the early Chevrolets had six-cylinder engines, and even a V-8 around 1917. But these larger engines were dropped when GM decided the best place for Chevrolet was the low-priced mass market.

Henry Ford for years had a virtual stranglehold on that market. It has been estimated that in 1920, half of all the cars on the road *in the entire world* were Model Ts.

When this photo was taken in 1919, Chevrolet was simply one of several makes trying to pull sales away from Ford. Ten years later, it was a different story. The Chevy went from four cylinders to six in 1929 — and this challenge prompted Henry Ford to terminate his Model A and bring out the first low-priced V-8 in 1932.

Going Nowhere Fast, 1920

WITH ALL THE BAD ROADS, even the best of cars broke down in the early days of motoring — including the Model T Ford shown here. But a broken axle was not a big problem. By 1920, Henry Ford had built several million Model Ts, and cheap replacement parts could be found at the nearest wrecking yard.

The Model T by this time was available with an electric starter, but that did not always guarantee the car would start. Cold winters were a problem, and ingenious methods were resorted to. One young man just east of Toronto took his girlfriend to a January dance. When he tried to drive her home, around midnight, his T refused to start because the carburetor was iced up. He told her to look the other way, then he opened the hood, climbed up onto a front fender, and urinated all over the fuel line leading to the carburetor. This bold and daring action melted the ice, the car started, and the young man drove his girlfriend home in what could rightly now be called a Model "P".

Railway Station, Ayton, circa 1920

THE LATE EARL DOMM (1902–1994) grew up in Ayton, Ontario, and this photo comes from his family album. Taken around 1920, it shows this 1915 Chalmers touring parked at the Ayton railway station with a man standing atop a rear fender, apparently reading the printing on either side of "Ayton" (the train schedule?). As a young lad, Earl saw boxcars full of unassembled Model T Fords unloaded onto the station platform, where the local Ford dealer and his helpers bolted them together and then drove them from the station to the local Ford garage. This spectacle (which always attracted a crowd) probably took place prior to 1913, when Henry Ford began using an assembly line.

Licensed As a Motorcycle, 1922

FRANK JAMES AND HIS DAUGHTER Doris are ready to go for a spin in this apparently homemade vehicle. It has four wheels (five if we count the driving wheel) and a steering wheel, but not much of a body beyond the two seats. Judging by the plates, it was licensed as a motorcycle. The four main wheels and tires were probably borrowed from a pair of bicycles.

"Buy Your Tires Here!" 1921

THIS LITTLE FRAME HOUSE AT 2486 Yonge Street in North Toronto may have been someone's home at one time. It was certainly part of the automotive scene when this photo was taken on November 22, 1921. Note the spark plug sign on the corner of the building. The large brick building in the background is the Capitol Theatre at Yonge and Castlefield, still there today, as an "event theatre." In 1921, movies were silent, and sound effects were often supplied by a piano player who tickled the ivories in tune with the action on the screen. Note the Model T Ford touring parked beside the theatre.

"Slow Down and Live" 1922

THIS PHOTO APPEARED IN THE *Toronto Globe* on December 5, 1922, with this explanation: "Summary justice for speed fiends is forecast in this placard, one of two placed yesterday near the entrance to Stanley Barracks (Exhibition Grounds), where Corporal Taylor was injured last week. Taylor's comrades give due and sufficient warning to careless drivers."

In 1984, the Ontario Ministry of Transportation and Communication published a book entitled *Footpaths to Freeways* to celebrate the bicentennial of the province. The little chapter on speed traps provides some interesting reading:

Screeching around a deep bend in the road, raising

choking clouds of dust, travelling a staggering 20 mph, the high-performance automobile of 1902 ate up the miles. Piloted by a speed-demon with maniacal gleam in his eye, this awesome engineering marvel defied anything in its path …

In 1903, when public protests against the dangerous speeds attained by automobiles had become an uproar, the provincial government was forced to take action.

No longer could motorists travel at breakneck speeds up to 20 mph along the province's roadways. A maximum speed limit of 15 mph was established, and somewhat drastic measures taken to enforce it.

The first step was to determine whether or not a driver was in fact speeding. One method was for two constables, placed one-tenth of a mile apart, to clock each other using a stop-watch.

Considerably more difficult was stopping the vehicle.

One simple, inescapable device for stopping speeders was a chain pulled taut across the road, firmly attached to two sturdy trees.

Yet another method was to throw a plank, studded with nails, in the path of an oncoming motorist. If he stopped before reaching the plank, he was driving within the speed limit, and was free to continue. If not, at the very least he got a flat tire for his trouble.[6]

"Toronto Welcomes You" 1924

WOODEN SIDEWALKS AND HOMEMADE TRAILERS were features of everyday life when John Boyd snapped this photo near the Humber River on Sunday, August 10, 1924. The car pulling the trailer is a four-door sedan, a body style that steadily gained in popularity throughout the 1920s.

Repair Garage, Beeton, 1925

DAVID HOOVER WROTE:

This is the interior of J.E. Rowes Garage on the main street of Beeton, Ont., on April 29, 1925 (a Wednesday). The men in the photo are, left to right, Jack McMinn, Dick Humphries, Wallace Hoover and Russell Alan. The Model T centre door belonged to Matthew Martin. Wallace Hoover (my grandfather) later bought his own garage down the street from Rowes in 1931 and operated it until his retirement in 1974.

"Your Money Is Safe in Here" 1925

THIS ARMOURED VEHICLE IS PARKED at a "No Parking" sign in front of the Bank of Montreal at Yonge and Front streets in Toronto on Tuesday, July 7, 1925. Note the modern-looking rear fender. A Model T Ford is parked behind. The fellow at the entrance to the bank looks suspicious. Perhaps a heist is about to happen. The building across the street (later demolished) was the headquarters of what is now the Toronto Transit Commission (affectionately known to Torontonians as the TTC). The bank now houses the Hockey Hall of Fame.

Camping at Point Pelee National Park, 1925

ONE OF THE SMALLEST IN all of Canada at six square miles, Point Pelee National Park in southwestern Ontario is the most southerly piece of mainland in this country. Visitors who enter the park immediately cross the forty-second parallel of latitude. All land south of this line is farther south than the northern boundary of California.

The car is a Chevrolet touring (note "bow tie" insignia on rad shell). Note the two-tone paint (black fenders with a body in colour). The growing popularity of two-tone cars in the 1920s made the black Model T Fords look increasingly dull and old-fashioned. Some of the last Model Ts were two-tone in a bid to stay competitive.

When this photo was taken in 1925, people often camped inside the park during the summer, and many wooden frame cottages were there as well. Today, all the cottages are gone in keeping with the current policy of the federal government in protecting and preserving the natural beauty of the park.

The man standing is Cole Cullen, who for many years operated Cullen Monuments in nearby Leamington. The young man in the car is the author's father, Frank T. Sherk, a factory worker at the H.J. Heinz Company in Leamington who rose through the ranks to become president of Heinz for all of Canada.

Margaret Baltzer

1927 Model T Roadster, Pelee Island, 1927

EIGHTEEN-YEAR-OLD NEIL QUICK smiles with pride behind the wheel of his new 1927 Model T Ford roadster. Working the family farm on Pelee Island with his father and selling muskrat pelts to a Toronto furrier, Neil was able to save enough money for his first car. Could this be the same car he used for "rum-running" to the United States during the days of Prohibition? Neil's daughter, Margaret Baltzer (née Quick), wrote:

> In his later years, my dad confessed to me that he "ran rum" across the Windsor-Detroit border during Prohibition but he would only take 11 bottles hidden inside the seat — because if they caught you with a case (12 bottles) they could impound your car. He also admitted to once attempting to

cross from Pelee Island to Sandusky, Ohio, on the ice but turned around when he heard shots fired.

So much illegal alcohol crossed from Windsor to Detroit in those days, the Detroit River was known as Rum Alley. The sale and manufacture of alcohol was prohibited in the U.S. under the Volstead Act (the eighteenth amendment) from 1919 to 1933. In Canada, Prohibition was a provincial responsibility — and Ontario experimented with it from 1919 to 1927.

Although the sale and consumption of alcohol was forbidden in Ontario during those years, it was still legal to manufacture it. This meant Canadians could supply their thirsty American cousins with an almost limitless supply of illegal alcohol. One of Canada's best customers was Chicago gangster Al Capone.

"Where's My Car?" 1926

FEW PICTURES ILLUSTRATE THE PROSPERITY of the 1920s better than this one, looking south toward Lake Ontario across a sea of cars parked beside Maple Leaf Stadium in 1926. Many of these cars were owned by people who had never owned a car before, and many deal-ers offered free driving lessons to close a sale. Just west of Bathurst Street and Lake Shore Boulevard, Maple Leaf Stadium was the home of Toronto baseball for forty-two years. It was torn down in 1968, long before the Blue Jays had a chance to play there.

Glenbow — Alberta Institute

Emancipated Woman Driving Studebaker Roadster, Alberta, circa 1926

IT TOOK A WORLD WAR to convince Canadian men to extend the right to vote to Canadian women. Manitoba became the first province to grant women this right, on January 27, 1916. Saskatchewan followed about two months later, and Alberta a few weeks after that. Ontario women joined their ranks on April 12, 1917. Winning the right to vote in federal elections took longer. Robert Borden's Conservative government passed the Wartime Elections Act in 1917 to gather support for its policy of conscription. This act gave the vote to wives, widows, mothers, sisters, and daughters of Canadian soldiers serving overseas. When the war reached its final year, Canadian men finally recognized the outstanding contribution to the war effort made by Canadian women. Their struggle for the right to vote achieved total victory by May 24, 1918.

With the battle for voting finally won, Canadian women began playing a more active role in everyday life. More women than ever before were driving cars — and car companies increasingly aimed their advertising at women. The woman seen here driving a Studebaker roadster near Cochrane, Alberta, in about 1926, reflected the growing emancipation women were beginning to enjoy.

Adrian Clements

GM Expands its Line of Cars

ADRIAN CLEMENTS OF SARNIA, ONTARIO, wrote: "1927 Pontiac coupe with Nan Catchpole (my grandmother), Betty (my mother), and Gordon (my uncle). Photo taken summer of 1930."[7]

General Motors introduced the Pontiac in 1926 as a companion car to the Oakland. In 1927 the LaSalle was introduced by GM as a companion car to the Cadillac. By 1929, Buick had the Marquette and Oldsmobile had the Viking. The only GM car not given a companion car in the 1920s was Chevrolet.

This proliferation of models reflected the thinking of GM president Alfred P. Sloan, who wanted to offer a car for every pocketbook. The onset of the Great Depression changed everything. The Marquette and Viking were gone by 1931, the Oakland disappeared in the early 1930s, and LaSalle was dropped at the end of 1940.

The Pontiac is unique in being the companion car that survived.

Jim Domm

Visitors to Canada, circa 1928

EARL DOMM (1902–1994) LIVED IN Toronto for most of his life, and for many years he was employed as the chief chemist of the Imperial Paint Company. In the late 1920s he worked for the Pierce-Arrow Motor Car Company in Buffalo, New York. His office was next to the area in the factory where the headlight housings were hammer-welded onto the front fenders (a design unique to Pierce-Arrow for many years). Even in his nineties, Mr. Domm said he could still hear the noise from all that hammering.

By 1929 he had moved back home to Toronto, driven there by a friend who owned a snazzy green 1927 Essex boattail speedster.

He brought with him a handful of paint stripers from the Pierce-Arrow factory. These little devices contained a small amount of paint and a little revolving wheel, and were used in the factory to pinstripe by hand the new Pierce-Arrows before they were shipped off to their new owners. These little paint stripers had the initials "P-A" moulded onto them.

Sixty years after leaving the Pierce-Arrow factory, Earl Domm was treated to a ride along the highway north of Whitby, Ontario, in Ron Fawcett's beautifully restored 1918 Pierce-Arrow. Ron began rebuilding cars as far back as 1942, and today he is probably the world's number-one restorer of Pierce-Arrows. In appreciation for the ride, Earl gave Ron the paint stripers from the Pierce-Arrow factory. Now, when Ron restores a Pierce-Arrow, he pinstripes the car with the very same device that pinstriped that car when it was new.

Earl Domm made many friends during the two years he worked at Pierce-Arrow in Buffalo, and he photographed the three American friends we see here who visited Ontario at that time. This car (a 1927 Buick Model 26 Standard coupe) would have crossed the Peace Bridge from Buffalo, New York, to Fort Erie, Ontario. The bridge opened for traffic in 1927.

Top-down Motoring, 1929

THIS 1928 ESSEX SUPER SIX roadster was just one year old when photographed. It has all the ingredients you need for sporty transportation: running boards, a rumble seat, three-tone paint, a fancy rad cap, twelve-spoke wooden wheels, and a windshield you can fold flat for wind-in-your-hair driving. The Essex first appeared in 1919 as a moderately priced car built by the Hudson Motor Car Co. of Detroit, Michigan. Beginning in February 1932, Hudson and Essex cars were produced in Tilbury, Ontario, to supply the nearly six hundred dealers across the Dominion. This Essex was owned by Edward Herbert Metcalfe, who lived in Toronto and served as a financial adviser to the Massey-Harris Company.

The author obtained this photo in 1996 after taking an elderly Toronto neighbour, Ada Woodyer, for a ride in his 1947 Mercury convertible. During that ride, he asked her if she remembered a car called the Studebaker ("Oh, yes"), Hudson ("Yes"), LaSalle ("Yes"), and Hupmobile ("Yes, that too"). Then he decided to test her on a car that was rare even when new.

"Ada, do you remember a car called the Cord?"

"Oh yes," Ada replied. "My best friend's husband owned one."

It turned out that husband was George Metcalfe, and he had indeed owned a front-wheel-drive Cord in Toronto in the early 1930s. He passed away several years ago, but Ada put the author in touch with his son, Ron Metcalfe, who lives today in Bramalea, Ontario. Ron has many photos of old cars in the Metcalfe family album, including the 1928 Essex Super Six roadster shown here. And here's the moral of this story: never underestimate what you can learn by talking to a senior citizen.

Did This Car Get a Parking Ticket? circa 1930

HERE WE ARE IN DOWNTOWN Toronto circa 1930. We're looking east on King Street West between Bay and York. In the background on the south side of the street can be seen the recently completed thirty-six-storey Canadian Imperial Bank of Commerce Building, which for many years was the tallest building in the British Commonwealth.

In the foreground and parked by the curb is a 1928 Chrysler roadster with two-tone paint and dual sidemounts. Note the rear-view mirrors mounted on top of the front fenders. Note also the partially open cowl vent in front of the windshield, a handy feature on a warm day.

Two features appearing together on this Chrysler clearly identify it as a 1928: the heavily curved rad shell and the two-piece front bumper that spreads apart in the middle. The design of the rad shell had remained essentially unchanged since the introduction of the Chrysler in 1924. The split-angled front bumper was new for 1928, and was carried over into 1929. But by that time the Chrysler rad shell had been redesigned.

The photograph itself comes from the Baldwin Room on the fourth floor of the Toronto Reference Library at 789 Yonge Street.

The Baldwin Room contains thousands of old historic photos of the Toronto area, and many of these photos are arranged alphabetically by street name. The photo of the Chrysler roadster is listed under "King Street between Bay and York."

Now take a close look at the passenger-side front tire on the roadster. You can see a white chalk mark, the telltale sign of a police officer hoping to issue a parking ticket.

After a Snowstorm, 1929

WE ARE LOOKING SOUTH ALONG Simcoe Street from Richmond in downtown Toronto after a snowstorm in December 1929. Winter driving back then could be hazardous, prompting many motorists to put their cars up on blocks till spring. This took the weight off the tires and prevented "flat spots" and the cracking of the sidewalls. They also drained the rad and engine block to avoid water freezing in the cooling system.

For those hardy motorists who insisted on driving through a Canadian winter some seventy-odd years ago, tire chains were a must. They were hard on the tires and hard on the roads and made quite a racket when driving on dry pavement. The modern snow tire has made them obsolete.

To defrost the windshield, many motorists lit a candle and mounted it on the dashboard. These candles would tip over on cornering, setting the mohair upholstery on fire. Hand-operated windshield wipers meant the driver had to plough through a snowstorm with only one hand on the wheel. The narrow tires gave poor traction, and motorists back then often carried along a snow shovel (not a bad idea even today). When you did get stuck in the snow, you could usually count on someone yelling, "Get a horse!"

Repair Garage, Toronto, circa 1930

CENTRAL CITY TIRE & BATTERY SERVICE was located at 5 Yorkville Avenue, just east of Yonge and north of Bay in midtown Toronto. It was well named because it was probably in the geographical centre of the city when this photo was taken around 1930. The sign on the wall refers you to 1276 Bay Street if you're in need of gas or oil.

Ron Ploder

Model A Fords in Family Album

HENRY FORD USED UP SEVERAL letters of the alphabet (including A, B, C, F, K, N, R, and S) before he hit upon the "universal car" of his dreams, the Model T. By 1927, the Model T was out of date after more than fifteen million had been built. Moving back to the front of the alphabet, Henry launched his new 1928 Model A in December 1927. It remained in production for four model years (1928–1931) and endeared itself to millions of motorists who bought and drove it.

Ron Ploder of Newmarket, Ontario, wrote:

My father was very popular in the 1930s as he was the only one with a car. His first car was a '28 Model A roadster and he enjoyed summer picnics [with it] in the Caledon Hills. He then bought a '29 and he and my uncles ('The Boys') posed with it at Queen's Park in Toronto. His last Model A was a 1930 roadster and I can remember riding in the rumble seat. What a thrill it was![8]

Downtown Traffic, Toronto, 1929

It's 3:20 P.M. ON SATURDAY, November 9, 1929, and we are looking south from Wilton Square down Yonge Street in Toronto.

Note the streetcar tracks, removed many years later when the city opened its first subway (March 30, 1954). Many interesting signs line the street. Note the Pantages Theatre on the left and Dallard's Ready-to-Wear on the right. A fellow with a sandwich board ad is just behind the parked car on the left. And the car making a left turn is a Model A Ford.

A New Brunswick Model A

IN 1994 GAR DARROCH OF Burlington, Ontario, purchased an extremely well-preserved 1931 Model A Ford Deluxe roadster with just 38,000 original miles. Evidence indicates that this roadster was never winter-driven. The doors fit and close like a 1931 showroom example. It has never suffered rust or collision damage. Even the frame has no pits! The fender beads are perfect. The engine's compression is like new, and the engine has never been restored. It was assembled at the Toronto Ford plant in the late winter or early spring of 1931. Its exceptional condition inspired Darroch to learn about its past.

After more than five years of extensive research, including travel to both the west and east coast as well as national newspaper advertising, some remarkable information has been discovered.

Darroch's roadster was sold new by Sussex Motors in Sussex, New Brunswick. The salesman who sold the car was Frank Coyle. The person he sold the car to was then fifty-eight-year-old Ada Gertrude Titus-Lake (1873–1964) of Sussex. Ada was a private duty nurse who worked in Brookline, Massachusetts. She returned to Sussex for the summer months. The roadster was for her summer transportation only. When she returned to the Boston area in September, she had the roadster professionally prepared for winter storage in her home's garage. Gar has met and become a friend of Roy Carhart, a mechanic who began maintaining Ada's roadster in 1940. Ada married George Lake in 1920. The marriage did not last

long and she had no children. She pampered this vehicle, the one car she owned in her lifetime, until she was eighty-one years old.

Gar's research has included documenting the memories of Ada's many friends who were children at that time. These individuals are now in their senior years. They recall Ada's kindness to them and being taken for rides in her car. The favourite seat for them was the rumble seat. One telephone call to Gar from New Brunswick began with the statement, "I carried groceries from your car into Ada's house many times when I was a boy."

Although Ada died thirty-seven years ago, some of her records have survived and are now in Gar's collection. These include a beautiful example of her signature. When she died in 1964, her two photograph albums were sent to her surviving sister in Vancouver. Sadly, these photo albums went missing in 1989 after being handed down through two more generations of family relations.

Reduced to looking for other surviving photographs from the descendants of her family relations and descendants of her friends, Gar has nonetheless found success. In what can only be described as miraculous discoveries, he has unearthed two photographs of Ada and the roadster together. The first was located in 1997 during a trip to Burnaby, British Columbia. It shows Ada sitting on the running board when the car was nearly new. She is with

friends in this lovely, unposed captured moment. The second was discovered in Vermilion, Alberta, in April of 1999. It shows Ada in 1952 standing beside the still pristine twenty-one-year-old roadster while parked beside the general store where she shopped.

Fortunately, the four owners from 1954 onward took good care of Ada's car for the next forty years. Gar has now owned it for nearly ten years and he gives it the care and attention it so richly deserves.

Many thanks to the Historic Automobile Society of Canada's *Klaxon* magazine, Winter 2001 issue, for the foregoing information.

Previous page: Ada sitting on the running board when her car was nearly new.

Above: Ada with the roadster in 1952 in front of the general store where she shopped.

Below: Ada's car today with Gar Darroch.

Car Races Train and Wins, Quebec, circa 1930

A DETAILED MESSAGE WAS WRITTEN in French on the back of this photo. Translated into English by Robbie Marchand, the message reads:

> Returning from a drive in the car with Uncle Alphonse and Aunt Simone on a beautiful Sunday afternoon where we were almost killed. Crossing bells were ringing, and the train was blowing its whistle. Suddenly Uncle Alphonse decides to step on the gas to pass in front of the train. The train misses the "rumble seat" by about two inches where the five of us were crammed in while Helen was in the front with Uncle and Aunt. Back home seated on the running board for the photograph I was still trembling. After the photograph, we went inside to tell our parents what Uncle Alphonse had done. This was our first and last car ride with him.

The young girl seated on the running board ("le marche-pied") apparently wrote the story of the race with the train many years after it happened — so many years in fact that she writes "1929 ou 1930" at the top and "1930?" at the end.

The photo was likely taken in Montreal. The balcony in front of the pair of doors on the second floor has an ornate wrought iron railing leading to an outdoor spiral staircase down to ground level. This was a popular architectural feature in older neighbourhoods of Montreal — and a practical feature as well. By having the staircase outside, more living space is created inside.

As to the make and year of the car, Don McArthur of Wasaga Beach, Ontario, wrote: "It is hard to identify a car of this era without seeing the radiator shell, but my best guess is that this sporty little car is a 1929 Studebaker Dictator cabriolet."

New Car Dealership, Toronto, 1931

Blythwood Motors opened as a Hudson-Essex dealership at Blythwood Road and Yonge Street in the heart of North Toronto in 1931. In December of that same year, Hudson-Essex of Canada Limited was formed to assemble their cars in Tilbury, Ontario. The actual assembly of vehicles (which began in February 1932) was performed by the Canadian Top and Body Company of Tilbury. Hudson merged with Nash in 1954 to form American Motors.

Barney Oldfield Comes to Toronto, 1931

BARNEY OLDFIELD BECAME A HOUSEHOLD name in 1902 when he raced Henry Ford's "999" at the Grosse Pointe track near Detroit. He won, and the publicity generated by that victory helped to launch the Ford Motor Company the following year. In that same year, 1903, Oldfield roared around the dirt oval at Indianapolis in the "999" racer he had bought from Henry Ford, and reportedly became the first man to go a mile a minute.

He retired from racing in 1918 but continued his interest in cars throughout his retirement years. On a return visit to Toronto in 1931 (he raced there in 1904), Oldfield, with cigar, was photographed behind the wheel of this new 1931 Hudson boattail speedster (he also attended the official opening of Blythwood Motors). This Hudson speedster was powered by a straight eight engine. Note placement of the horn in front of the rad and the fancy tire cover on the fender-mounted spare.

City of Toronto Archives, TTC Series 71, #8399

Remember Tree-lined Streets?

MANY CITY STREETS ACROSS CANADA years ago were shaded by a large green canopy of trees planted on both sides. Unfortunately, as streets were widened to accommodate a growing number of cars, the existing trees were chopped down and — all too often — never replanted further back. This view of Spadina Avenue in Toronto (looking north to Queen) on March 10, 1931, shows trees that grew right on the street.

Ed Janzen

Model T Coupe, Manitoba, 1932

Ed Janzen of Belwood, Ontario, wrote:

My father's first car was a Model T Ford Coupe. This car was purchased from a garageman (this is how my father called him) on the day my mother arrived with me only one month old in her arms. She had come all the way from Manitou, Manitoba on the train (some 120 miles). I can imagine the surprise on my mother's face when Dad told her he had bought a car just to take us home to the teacherage in Arborg, a village some 35 miles away.

Surprise may have quickly turned to chagrin when Mom found out that Dad had only a few minutes driving experience and this was acquired driving out to meet us at the train station.

Dad still remembers the Model T with fond memories because he says it served us well. Since Dad isn't particularly adept at mechanical things, he has always valued trouble-free transportation.

After a couple of years, my parents moved to a school called Felsendorf which was a little closer to civilization and only six miles from Gimli. I can still remember the long rides from Gimli to Winnipeg to see my cousins in the big city. Sitting on the floor of the coupe (my sister, three years younger, had priority on my mother's lap) I could hear the rhythmic unending ZZ-ZZ-ZZ-ZZ of what must have been the planetary gears (the Model T Ford transmission). Since the car was bought in 1932, it could not have been too old (from a photograph I guess the T was a '26 or '27 model).

I don't remember if my parents drove the car in winter but I do recall the frequent trips to Gimli for groceries in the summer. My father had a sweet tooth and he always remembered to bring us something. An O'Henry chocolate bar was (and still is) his favourite. I also remember the licorice ropes, the beige-orange "peanuts" and the bright red "strawberries."

In the summer the T carried the family to Gimli more often because Dad loved to swim and Lake Winnipeg had some wonderful beaches. The road leading past the school and to Gimli was a gravelled well-travelled highway (for those days) and I don't recall that it ever suffered from rain. Dad loved to go for short rides, either to explore new roads or to stop in and visit with the families living in the school district he served as a teacher. The people were friendly, out-going and hospitable. We would always come back with a load of vegetables and farm produce received as gifts from our neighbours.

The photo of the T shows my father, with my sister on his knee and me sitting on the running board.[9]

Dennis Pascoe

Ivor Pascoe's Model A Ford

IT ALL BEGAN IN A coal mine in Wales over seventy years ago. Ivor Pascoe, age twenty, had been working underground since he was fourteen, and he had finally decided there had to be a better life somewhere else. After taking a short agricultural course, he said goodbye to his father and his many brothers and sisters and boarded the S.S. *Arcania* leaving from Southampton on May 18, 1929. He was on his way to Canada.

He laboured on a farm for a year, then headed off to Toronto to seek his fortune.

At first, living on Dufferin Street, he survived with odd jobs (the Depression was now underway), and one of these jobs involved driving a Model T fruit truck that he kept on the road by crawling underneath it every night to make repairs. Then he was hired as a driver for Dufferin coal and had a steady job.

Fortune was now smiling on Ivor in more ways than one. In his spare time, he attended the U.B. Church and U.B. Mission ("U.B." standing for United Brethren, a group descended from Pennsylvania Mennonites). Ivor was not a Mennonite, but he attended because these two churches were close to where he lived. And it was through the U.B. Church that Ivor met and married his wife, Florence (her father had immigrated to Toronto around 1906 from the rough, east-end docklands of London). They both had a lot of friends at both U.B. churches and would often go to both on various occasions.

They tied the knot on January 2, 1932, and celebrated their sixtieth wedding anniversary in 1992.

Shortly after they were married, they were photographed beside their car, a second-hand Model A Ford coach. Although the car appears to be the Standard model rather than the Deluxe (judging by the single spare tire on the rear instead of twin sidemounts in the front fenders), Ivor is bursting his buttons with pride as he smiles at the camera with his new bride. Running boards came in handy at a time like this, making it possible for even the shortest of men to stand tall. And to think this young man had been working in a Welsh coal mine just a few years earlier!

Dennis Pascoe

A VERY DAPPER IVOR PASCOE poses with the old Chev truck that he drove for Nash Haulage in 1932.

Mayfair Magazine, July 1935

Styling in Search of Sales

THE THREE GRAHAM BROTHERS — JOSEPH, Robert, and Ray — made a name for themselves by building trucks in the 1920s. In 1927, they purchased the faltering Paige-Detroit Car Company and began building cars bearing their name the following year. They were called Graham-Paiges through 1930 and Grahams after that. Nearly eighty thousand Graham-Paiges were built and sold in 1929, thanks to the tide of prosperity that pushed total North American car production close to five million, a record high for that time.

The stock market crash in October 1929 and the onset of the Great Depression changed everything. Several well-known makes disappeared (Durant, Marmon, Auburn, Cord, and Franklin, to name a few) while the ones that survived faced a long struggle against plummeting sales and rivers of red ink. In 1932, Packard introduced its Light Eight to move down-market to capture more sales, only to discover the move cost seven million dollars because it pulled sales away from the bigger, more profitable Packards.

At first glance, it seems ironic that some of the greatest engineering and styling advances in the automobile took place during the most economically depressed decade of the twentieth century — the 1930s. And yet it could hardly have been otherwise. In the frantic scramble for customers, the car companies had to produce cars that looked new and performed better than ever before.

In January 1932, Graham introduced the Blue Streak Eight with sensational styling that still looks good over seventy years later. But sales remained low, and Graham kept losing money. Only a few 1941 models were build before production ended in late 1940.

Some Grahams were built in Canada from 1931 to the mid-1930s. The stylish Graham convertible coupe shown here was owned by Mrs. Albert U. Cote, photographed beside her car while on her way to the Toronto Golf Club.

Glen Ubelacker

Glen Ubelacker's 1932 Oldsmobile Convertible, Wasaga Beach, circa 1941

THIS CAR CAME INTO GLEN'S life in 1939, when he was sixteen years old. Here is how it happened …

Glen's first car was a 1926 or '27 Dodge coupe acquired through his dad as a trade-in at Beattie Cadillac in downtown Toronto. It had four bald tires, which Glen replaced with a set of used, recut, oversized tires — but the car still road like a buckboard. To jazz it up a little, Glen got an artist to paint "The Jitterbug" in big yellow letters on the black spare tire cover at the back.

However, Glen knew from day one that this car did not properly reflect his *joie de vivre* personality. In fact, on the very first day he drove it to the family home on Poplar Plains Crescent near Avenue Road and St. Clair in midtown Toronto, he noticed that the two girls who lived across the street tittered and sniggered at the sight of his old car. This old Dodge would not be around for long.

On a warm, sunny day later that spring of 1939, Glen was driving with his sister Velma in the Dodge along St. Clair Avenue West.

92

Suddenly he spotted the car of his dreams: a yellow and black 1932 Oldsmobile convertible with twin horns, dual sidemounts, and lots of chrome. It was parked on a used car lot on the south side of St. Clair east of Oakwood. This car lot belonged to St. Clair-Oakwood Motors, a Dodge-DeSoto dealer with their showroom on the opposite side of the street.

Glen pulled in, traded off his Dodge on the spot, and drove the Olds home. When his dad saw it, he said, "Son, it's a beaut!"

Indeed it was. In addition to the features already mentioned, Glen's car had a folding trunk rack, a golf bag door on the passenger side, landau irons on the convertible top, roll-up windows, a fold-down windshield, a rumble seat, steel spoke wheels, and brown leather interior.

It did not have whitewall tires, but Glen fixed that right away. He rushed down to the big Canadian Tire store at Yonge and Davenport (which had opened two years earlier and is still there today) and bought a can of whitewall tire paint. The service was quick because the fellows in the stockroom wore roller skates.

Glen applied the tire paint with great care to fool everyone into thinking his whitewalls were genuine. The white tire paint quickly yellowed, and Glen applied a fresh coat every weekend. This tire paint was a permanent expense and so, to save money, Glen drove the car only on weekends.

Under the hood was a flathead six that cranked out 74-horsepower from 213 cubic inches. This engine dated back to 1928, when General Motors hired the worst drivers it could find to road-test the new F-28 Oldsmobiles. These tests resulted in a very rugged car, and this quality was still evident in Glen's car, which was built four years later.

And Glen's car had a feature not available in 1928: a transmission with synchromesh into second and high. Without having to double-clutch, Glen's arm could spend more time wrapped around his girlfriend.

It also had free-wheeling, a fad feature that faded out by the end of the year.

The more Glen drove his Olds, the farther afield he went. He was frequently seen pulling into the Shore View Drive-In Restaurant on Lakeshore Road near Mimico. You could drive down to the back of the restaurant to buy hot dogs and you could park close enough to the lake to put your front wheels in the water.

Wasaga Beach on Georgian Bay was a favourite destination for Glen and his '32 Olds. There was a dance hall and a snack bar, and people drove their cars right along the beach. Glen remembers one moonlit night when he and a girlfriend shared the front seat of the Olds while it was parked with its front wheels in the water.

The evening was very romantic until the end of Glen's cigarette fell off red-hot right onto his hand. He jumped out and plunged his hand into the waters of the bay. The romantic mood quickly returned as his girlfriend gave him lots of sympathy.

Between 1941 and 1943, Glen was employed at Research Enterprises Ltd. on Vanderhoof Avenue, near Eglinton Avenue and Laird Drive in Leaside. For part of his time there, Glen was still driving the Olds, and he went all over the city procuring engineering equipment for the war effort at R.E.L. (where they were building radar equipment and other essential items).

The Olds still ran well, but the top was bad. It was probably the original top, and the car was now nearly ten years old. Glen recalls the time it rained non-stop for three days and he, being a gentleman, gave a ride home to a woman who worked at R.E.L. She was wearing a beige coat and she sat in the front seat, which Glen had covered with a Royal Stewart plaid automobile rug.

The rain, the rug, and the beige coat turned out to be an unfortunate combination. When she climbed out, she discovered the back of her beige coat was now Royal Stewart plaid.

"I'll never ride with you again," she snapped, then slammed the door.

Glen's Olds was still sharp and flashy after ten years on the road — and that was the problem. Glen was now nearly twenty years old (almost an old man!) and he began thinking that an old yellow convertible was no longer appropriate in his new role as parts procurer for such a highly respected firm as R.E.L.

He took his '32 Olds to Grieve Motors on Roncesvalles Avenue and traded it for a much more conservative 1936 Chev sedan. He never saw the Olds again.

Bill Sherk

Author with Glen Ubelacker

THE LATE GLEN UBELACKER (RIGHT) and author Bill Sherk were photographed at a Thornhill Cruise Night around 1996. They are sitting on the running board of a 1932 Chevrolet cabriolet — a car very similar to the '32 Olds Glen had owned over fifty years earlier.

National Archives of Canada, PA #68162, Peake & Whittingham Collection

Car Wash, Toronto, 1933

THIS PHOTO WAS LIKELY TAKEN at a dealership with the car wash area partitioned off. The car being washed has a red metal triangle attached to the left rear fender. It says "Four Wheel Brakes" and warns other motorists not to tailgate. Many cars had only two-wheel brakes until the late 1920s. Buick adopted four-wheel brakes in 1924 after two and a half years of research and 150,000 miles of road testing. Note the sporty 1931 Chevrolet roadster with dual sidemounts and fold-down windshield.

Keith Thomson

Nova Scotia Snowstorm, 1934

KEITH THOMSON OF FREDERICTON, NEW Brunswick, wrote:

Even with chains it was a long ten mile trip from Greenfield to Truro, N.S., in the winter of '34 with the new '34 Ford. At left is the late Sandy MacKenzie and right is the late Harold Thomson, who remembered the situation clearly. Taking the picture was Eleanor Keith, now Mrs. Harold Thomson.[10]

1934 Ford Deluxe Sedan Delivery

Gord Hazlett of Old Autos newspaper wrote:

This photo was lent to me by Tony Bondi of Bondi's Auto Service in Aurora one day when I was in getting my truck serviced. This picture was taken at Sunnyside Beach in Toronto in 1934 and shows Tony's brother, Paul, playing in the sand and his grandmother, Gatto, maybe getting the picnic lunch ready at the rear. The sidemount, the special wheels, the oversized tires, with, I guess a flathead V8, would make this vehicle a real deluxe model. (Who wouldn't give his eye tooth to own such a model today?) Tony's dad, Frank, owned and operated "Bondi's Better Bananas" business from #25 Church St. until

1957. After this vehicle he bought a Studebaker truck from Logan Motors on Queen St. East. Sorry to say Frank Bondi passed away in 1996 but reached the great age of 92. I met this lovely old gentleman at Tony's garage a few years ago and rehearsed a few old stories about the Toronto of years ago. He remembered a lot of the old firms that did business around the St. Lawrence Market selling fruit and vegetables wholesale. These firms, like Bondi's Bananas have all been long gone. Pity. Well sir, when you read where old established companies like T. Eaton Company are in trouble you can believe anything. Both Frank and I enjoyed our chat. I'll look you up Frank when my time comes, but don't rush me.[11]

National Archives of Canada, PA #133371

No Grease Pit Here, Quebec, 1934

IT'S FRIDAY, JUNE 15, 1934, and someone's new 1934 Ford cabriolet is up on the hoist at Laurentide Automobiles Inc. in Quebec City. Many, if not most, service garages back then had a grease pit for oil changes and lubrication and general repairs. This place was state-of-the-art for 1934, the latest equipment and something to be proud of.

Miss Doris Neale, 65 Castlefrank Road, Toronto, and her Hupmobile "8" cabriolet equipped with Goodyear Heavy Duty Tires.

DISTINGUISHED!

Immediately set apart from all other tires by the clean-cut All-Weather tread, Goodyear Heavy Duty Tires possess a distinction not shared by any other make.

All over the world the All-Weather Tread is the mark of the most distinguished of all automobile tires. Most fine cars are Goodyear-equipped, because no other tire has attained to that all-round perfection which, for 19 consecutive years has given Goodyear undisputed leadership.

GOODYEAR

Canadian Homes and Gardens, April 1934

Goodyear and Hupmobile, 1934

HOW TIMES HAVE CHANGED! BACK in 1934, a single woman (Miss Doris Neale) who owned a flashy red convertible (a Hupmobile "8" cabriolet) didn't mind having a photo of herself and her car published in this magazine ad; the photo was taken in front of her home, with her Toronto address (65 Castle Frank Road) included in the ad.

The Hupp Motor Car Company was born on Monday, November 8, 1909, one week after Robert C. Hupp finished building his first Model 20 runabout. Hupmobiles were well built and moderately priced and sold well until the Depression of the 1930s.

Doris Neale's cabriolet was the product of a company desperately struggling to survive in the fiercely competitive automotive market. Their slogan for 1938 ("Step Up with a Hupp") failed to reverse the downward slide, and production ended forever in October 1940, just three weeks after the start of the 1941 models.

Springtime on Bay Street, Toronto, 1935

THE CAMERA IS LOOKING NORTH on Bay from Queen Street as springtime traffic rolls by. The City Hall (still there after more than one hundred years) is on the right. On the left is Shea's Hippodrome, scene of many vaudeville shows and Hollywood movies — here featuring "Easter Parade Revue." Shea's was torn down with the rest of that block in the late 1950s to clear the way for Nathan Phillips Square and Toronto's new City Hall. But Shea's survived long enough to show Elvis's first motion picture, *Love Me Tender*, released by 20th Century Fox in November 1956.

City of Toronto Archives, Fonds 1244, Item 7300

Old Autos

The Innocents Went West

The following condensed story was published in full in *Old Autos* in 1995:

On June 15, 1935, four young girls in their twenties bought an old Ford car for $50.00 and drove from London, Ontario, to Vancouver, B.C., and back. The four girls were Anne Simmons (Mrs. Cowhig), Eva Copeland (Mrs. Gordon Zurbrigg), Alicia Palmer (Mrs. Dr. Bev Robinson), and Marguerite Smith … This is Marguerite Smith's recollection, written in 1993, of an epic journey by four young girls in a Model T Ford Touring car.

"Now in my more cautious 85th year, I have no idea what could possibly have made us do such a thing! But this is how it happened:

"Anne's father owned a garage in Exeter, Ontario, and he was a shrewd mechanic who had an eye for a good deal. He took note of this particular 'Tin Lizzy' that came to his attention. The owner had been a man who took good care of his car; he took the wheels off and set the car up on blocks every winter, as some people did in those days. They had lots of snow around Exeter and it seems to have been a good idea! It had an engine that purred like a sewing machine, and now that the owner was selling it for $50.00, the garage man snapped it up. His daughter Anne, who was 23 and full of bright ideas, bought this car from her father and needed help in paying for it, so she talked two of her friends into becoming part owners. One idea led to another, and before long these three had decided to take a trip 'up west' and across Canada to Vancouver in it.

"We had all recently graduated from Victoria Hospital, London, as nurses, and it was the middle of the depression and there wasn't much work anyway. So, one day as I came out of the dining room at the hospital, these three girls surrounded me and said 'Smitty, how would you like to take a trip out west with us?' I told them I didn't have any money, but they assured me it wasn't going to cost that much. On the spur of the moment I said: 'Sure I'll go!' (I don't think I really meant it at the time, but once having said it, I felt I should keep my promise).

"Anne and Eva were learning to drive and by now knew enough to keep the car on the road. Alicia, like myself, had never driven a car, but when we had each paid our $12.50 for ownership of the car, we could legally say it was ours. Drivers were more or less self-taught in those days. We learned that our Ford had three pedals on the floor and an emergency brake. There were two little levers up on the wheel which were very important — one for the gas, the other the spark — and there was a crank at the front of the car. We knew how to open up the hood and look at our fine engine. The top had side curtains that would either stay up or come down in fine weather.

"Anne's father, Mr Simmons, seems to have been something of a 'fixer' and put the front seat on hinges so that it would recline if we needed a bed.

One plan led to another, and by the time I saw the car, it had a long cupboard built along one side on the running board between the two fenders to hold cooking utensils, food, etc. It had licence plate NB500 to attest to its great importance. Anne decided to call it 'Bearcat.'

"The girls had bought enough khaki coloured denim to make up two sets for each of shorts, shirts and wrap-around skirts, so we could dress according to the weather.

"We set June 15th as our take-off date and decided to meet at my parents' place near Watford, Ontario, as that was the last point west on our way to Sarnia, Ontario.

"We planned to cross the border from Sarnia to Port Huron on our way into Michigan, through Wisconsin, Minnesota and on to Winnipeg, Manitoba.

"Just at that time a little white fox terrier was lost and ended up at my parents' home. One of the girls got the bright idea that we needed a mascot, so the dog was named 'Paddy' and bundled into the car with the rest of us. It was a bright and sunny day when we took off for points west. My parents weren't very enthusiastic about our plans, but they were good sports about it all and went along with our plans. A group of neighbours and the minister and his family were there to see us off."

The four young women with the dog reached Sarnia, where they paid 90 cents to take the car ferry to Port Huron, Michigan. Not much sleep the first night camping ("murdering mosquitoes, quieting the pup and worrying about snakes").

By June 20 (a Thursday), the old Model T was chugging through northern Michigan: "Came to a log cabin plus two beds for $1.50 cash — right on the shore of Lake Superior at Ashland."

They reached Manitoba and spent a week in

Winnipeg with Eva's aunt and uncle. Then on to Saskatchewan, where they stopped to visit with various friends and relatives. Mr. Bennett (a friend of Anne's father) had his own garage "and he offered to give our car a free tune-up and overhauled it from stem to stern, oiled and replaced any worn parts — clutch band, brake band, reverse, new points and timer, 5 gals. Gas, 4 qts. Oil in car, 2 qts in can — and refused payment. He thoroughly inspected it and announced it as good as new."

Now they headed further west along dirt roads leading to the Saskatchewan-Alberta border. Then it started to rain. "We had been warned about Saskatchewan roads and were told that 'gumbo' roads developed into a mixture of grease and glue when it rained … Pretty soon we found that the car wouldn't stay on the road but slid from side to side and even in a circle. Since Alicia was driving, Anne, Eva, and I took off our wrap-around skirts and in our shorts and bare feet we got behind the car to hold it on the road. The wheels spun and the mud spattered up and all over us, and it was still raining!"

They dried off, cleaned up, and were fed at the home of Mr. and Mrs. H.E. King of Beadle,

Saskatchewan, who were thrilled to have them stop in.

On to Calgary, in time for the chuckwagon races and RCMP "Musical Ride" at the Calgary Stampede.

Then to Banff and Lake Louise and into the Rocky Mountains: "Our little 'Tin Lizzie' kept chugging along, sometimes climbing continually upwards for miles at a time. Now and then we would come to safe areas where we could stop and allow our engine to cool down. At times our radiator boiled and steam came out of the rad cap."

The mountain roads were mostly gravel with no guard rails: "On a bright and early morning I was driving and keeping well to the right of the road and as close to the edge of the cliff as I dared, when around the corner at a high rate of speed, and

in a cloud of dust, well over on my side of the road, hurtled a local car, probably late for work.

"Since I had no choice, I stood my ground, held my breath, and waited for the inevitable to happen. It didn't! Just at the last minute, with grav-

el flying, he turned his car back into his own lane and missed us by inches."

They kept going, trying to admire the spectacular scenery while driving along gravel roads "so crooked it would break a snake's back."

Finally Vancouver, where they stayed with Eva's Aunt Gertie: "She was a widow with a big house and a big heart and she welcomed us with open arms."

Finally it was time to head home. Their return journey took them through Yellowstone Park in Wyoming, where they had more adventures. And at long last, after eight weeks on the road, that old 50-dollar Model T Ford brought them all the way back to Ontario and home. "What great fun it had been. But later on, when some of my friends said they would like to do the same thing, I always said: 'Don't do it. You will never make it. We were just lucky.' (And so we were.)"[12]

Downtown Traffic, 1935

WE ARE LOOKING SOUTH ON Yonge Street in downtown Toronto near Trinity Square in the early afternoon of Saturday, December 21, 1935. Shoppers crowd the street and sidewalks on this third-last shopping day before Christmas.

The parked car in the foreground (license HT.461) is a 1935 Ford convertible coupe or roadster with rumble seat (convertibles had roll-up windows; roadsters had side curtains). This was the last model year that Ford cars were equipped with wire wheels and the second-last model year with an exposed spare tire. The older car between the Ford and the streetcar tracks carries the new white-on-black 1936 plate (B.190), which probably went on sale Monday, December 2. The 1935 plates were black on orange.

Across the street is a 1934 Chrysler Airflow, an early but commercially unsuccessful attempt at streamlining. It is parked in front of Robinson's clothing store. Further down is the One Minute Lunch, an early participant in the fast-food business.

1934 Pontiac, 1936

Valerie Brook wrote:

Dear Mr. Sherk: Following your interesting presentation to the Swansea Historical Society, I got out the old family albums and found the enclosed photo of my grandfather and me in front of his Port Whitby home. Beside us is my Dad's car. The license plate is 1936 but we always had a second-hand car, usually old Pontiacs. I found a bill dated July 1935, showing the purchase by my father of a used 1934 Pontiac Deluxe sedan from Ontario Motor Sales in Oshawa for $650 plus his old '28 Essex sedan.

The Village of Swansea was (and is) very sandy and since Dad was an avid gardener, each time we visited my grandparents, we came home with two old potato bags full of their garden soil (on our bumper) to add to our sand. Grandfather had an acre with a chicken house at the rear end of his property.

Valerie Brook

A Tale of Two Running Boards

THE PHOTO ON THE LEFT was taken around 1924 near Leamington, Ontario. The fellow on the running board is Frank T. Sherk (1904–1972), about twenty years old at that time. The car is a Model T Ford roadster, and the side curtains offer only marginal protection from the winter weather. Note the impression left in the snow by the narrow tires, a far cry from the road-gripping wide-tread radials of today. Young Sherk is making good use of the running board as a place to pose while having his picture taken. The term "running board" dates back to at least 1825, when barges on the Erie Canal had boards along the side for crew members to walk along with poles to help the barge along. When they got to the end of the board, they ran to the other end with their pole.

The second photo was taken in 1936, about twelve years after the first. Frank Sherk this time is the photographer, and he is taking a picture of his pretty, young wife, Edna, alongside their new 1936 Ford two-door sedan en route to a holi-

day in the Maritimes. Car bodies by this time were wider and running boards were getting narrower. They could also be dust collectors and not a place for a young lady to sit while wearing a pretty white dress.

When Frank and Edna reached the Maritimes, they visited a coal mine on Cape Breton Island, descending deep into the earth and exploring a tunnel that extended out under the Atlantic Ocean. They also visited the famous Canadian schooner, the *Bluenose*, which sank in a storm in 1946 but is now immortalized on the Canadian dime. Their 1936 Ford, with its flathead V-8 engine, fabric insert roof, and mechanical brakes, performed flawlessly throughout the entire trip. They kept driving the '36 for the next four years, then traded it in for a new 1940 Mercury two-door sedan at the Riverdale Garage, a large Ford and Mercury dealer in Toronto. That's the year they were blessed with the birth of their first son, John, followed two years later by Bill, the author of this book.

Kent Weale

Harry Weale's 1935 Oldsmobile

HARRY WEALE AND HIS FUTURE bride Gladys (along with an unidentified rear seat passenger) were photographed with Harry's 1935 Oldsmobile coach at blossom time near Niagara-on-the-Lake in 1938. This was a new streamlined body for 1935, making the boxy-looking '34 models out of date. The 1935 and '36 Oldsmobiles were similar in appearance. The quickest way to tell them apart is the doors. The 1935s have rear-hinged "suicide doors." The '36s are hinged at the front.

The big news for Oldsmobile in 1935 was the new all-steel "turret top" that replaced the old fabric-insert design. Henry Ford claimed an all-steel roof produced a drumming noise on the highway, but he then switched to an all-steel roof in 1937.

Aside from leaking and needing periodic repair, the old fabric roofs had other drawbacks. Paul Calderone recalls his dad and uncle talking about the day they visited the St. Lawrence Market in downtown Toronto in the mid-1930s to buy fruit and vegetables to sell door-to-door. They hitched up their horse and wagon outside. When they came back, they discovered their horse had eaten a large portion of the fabric roof off a car parked nearby. The owner of the car was very upset, but Paul's dad and uncle had no money. All they could do was apologize, then clip-clop away.

Oldsmobiles in 1935 were available in a variety of colours, including black, maroon, grey, blue, red, and two greens. Like many Canadian motorists back then, Harry Weale's favourite car colour was a conservative black. It was the best choice for blending in with the rest of the traffic.

Kent Weale

Kent Weale's First Car

AT AGE SIXTEEN, IN 1960, Harry Weale's son Kent bought his first car: a 1940 Ford Deluxe coupe. He paid $200 for it and drove it home. When Dad came out to look at it, he saw four colours parked in his driveway: a black trunk lid, a grey body, doors, and hood, a pink roof with four pink fenders, and one whitewall tire.

This was not the colour scheme Harry Weale would have chosen. Imagine his relief when Kent repainted the car a light blue right at home with thirteen spray bombs from Canadian Tire. Still not a conservative black, but Dad now found the old car easier to tolerate. Kent owned it for the next two years — and one weekend, when his parents were away, he replaced the original flathead V-8 with a Buick V-8 engine. But that's another story for another book ...

Ervin Groening

Manitoba Farm, circa 1936

ERVIN GROENING OF WINKLER, MANITOBA, wrote:

The picture was at harvest time 1936 or 1937 (the license plate seems to be a "6"; in those days you got new plates every year and paid mostly for the actual plates themselves). The vehicle in the picture is a 1923 Hupmobile which my oldest brother cut down to create a semi-trailer tractor. As a touring car it had no trouble cruising at 60 mph which certainly wasn't what could really be said of Ford and Chevs of the same year. It also had more load pulling power than our 1 ton Fargo truck of 1929. The Hup engine was a long stroke 4 cylinder and very smooth and well balanced. I should mention too, that my brother reduced the rear wheel diameter for a better load-bearing tire.[13]

Andy Craig, Coquitlam, B.C.

Fraser Canyon Road, British Columbia

LLOYD BROWN WROTE:

This 1937 Federal truck with standard cab is hauling cargo through the British Columbia mountains along the Fraser Canyon Road. Federal built trucks from 1910 to 1959. During their lifetime they produced an estimated 160,000 units with a weight range from light duty 3/4 ton, through medium and heavy duty units to 20 tons. The Federal in this photo is one of the Vanderspeck fleet on the Fraser Canyon Road in British Columbia.[14]

On the Road in Quebec, circa 1938

JEAN MARCOUX OF MONT-SAINT-HILAIRE, Quebec, wrote:

In the March 3, 2003 edition of *Old Autos*, I read with interest your article titled "The car that raced the train and won". And to my surprise I recognized my own father, Robert, in the 1938 Ford picture. He died in 1983, but I showed it to my 93-year-old mother and she said: "Sure it's him!" [Photo purchased by author at Barrie Automotive Flea Market in spring of 1999.]

His name was Robert Marcoux. At that time he was living in Shawinigan, Que., and was a travelling salesman for UAP (United Auto Parts), and had to go by Ontario roads to reach Abitibi. Dad was a "car man." He loved cars since his father had the first car in Victoriaville, Que., in 1910. He even possessed a Stutz, circa 1935, that had served as a transport getaway car for bootleggers. It had a hidden tank to transport booze, but also a reservoir containing warm oil to shoot behind on the road to prevent the motorcycle policemen from chasing them (it would make the road slippery and the "spotter" on the motorcycle would get oil on his goggles!!!).

I am a car guy too. So is my son and his son. I've had many antiques. Since I dig "orphans," I presently have a 1953 Kaiser Manhattan and a 1954 Nash Ambassador 2-door hardtop fresh from Kamloops, B.C.

Gord Hazlett

Durant Roadster on Fishing Trip, 1937

GORD HAZLETT TELLS THE story:

This '29 Durant roadster was bought from Greenwood Auto Wreckers owner, Mitch Forbes, one of Mitch's "Greenwood Resales," by an old buddy of mine by the name of Jim McTavish. This was in 1937, and the price was $35.00 cash and it was McTavish's first car. He was 16 years old and had a steady job delivering for Dawes Bakery on Queen St. East in the beach district, on a bicycle of course. Jim lived at the corner of Ashdale Ave. and Applegrove and was very popular among his buddies because he had "wheels." I, at this time, had my own wheels, a '27 Chev coach. There were six or seven of us who used to chum together, namely, Jim McTavish, Harold and Albert Greer, Mel and Alf Brazier, Bill Tobutt and Yours Truly. We still all keep in touch but sad to say Bill Tobutt never made it back from overseas. He was killed in a Jeep accident, after V.E. day.

114

Jim had this car for some time and we used to go out to Frenchman's Bay fishing many times. (Note our bamboo fishing poles along the side of the car). I guess you question how we got six guys in a roadster? Three sat in the front, illegal in those days, and three sat in the trunk. We used to remove the trunk lid and sit with our feet hanging out the back. One day Albert Greer was learning to drive and pulled out onto #2 highway when he shouldn't have. We were nearly rear-ended and I remember us in the trunk pulling our legs up under our chins. I can still see the look of terror on that driver's face as he stood on the brakes of that Model A. And was he mad. He gave Albert a piece of his mind I'll tell you.

The end of the Durant came very suddenly one day when Bill Tobutt borrowed it to go up to Gerrard St. to the fish and chip store and on the way back down Ashdale he gunned the motor to attract some girls on the street, showing off, of course. This caper caused a con rod to go through the block. He walked up to my house to tell me the motor had stopped and could I come and see why. As soon as we started to walk down Ashdale the road was covered in oil. I said, "Bill it looks kind of serious and final." Sure enough when I opened the hood you could shake hands with the crankshaft without any trouble. Well sir, the next thing was to break the bad news to Jim, the proud owner. We hand pushed it into Jim's backyard. Jim took the news bravely as he was expecting it because he said it had this funny noise for a while. The neighbours came from miles around to see this sad car much as you would visit a patient in the hospital with a broken leg. Anyhow, Jim couldn't afford to repair the car and between the six of us we couldn't buy a shingle off a backhouse. The Durant went back to whence it came, Greenwood Auto Wreckers. Oh how I wish I could have bought it and saved it for my old age. Imagine a '29 Durant roadster for, I believe, Jim got $20.00 from Mitch. It makes me cry.[15]

Long Live the King! 1937

THE BIG NEWS ACROSS CANADA IN MAY 1937 was the coronation of King George VI following the abdication of Edward VIII the previous year. The Ontario government celebrated the event by issuing white-on-red 1937 license plates with a crown in each upper corner. These "twin-crown" plates were unique to that year (there has been a single crown ever since, except for 1951). Birks Jewellery Store on Yonge Street in Toronto mounted a huge crown over the entrance. Parked in front: a 1936 LaSalle rumble-seat convertible coupe and a 1937 Oldsmobile sedan with eye-level tail lights.

Don and Marilyn Prest are the proud owners of this immaculate 1937 Chrysler Airflow, photographed at the Pickering Museum in June 2003. Note twin crowns on 1937 Ontario plate.

British Columbia Convertible

GORDON WEBB OF CRANBROOK, BRITISH Columbia, owns a very rare Canadian-built 1937 Chevrolet cabriolet. This is its story as told by Gordon himself:

I believe it was purchased new in Vernon, B.C. by a woman and was traded in sometime in 1955. It was then purchased by a fellow who worked in a saw mill. I was working in a service station at the time and he used to purchase gas there in a small village called Barriere, B.C., which is about 40 miles north of Kamloops, B.C.

He ran it pretty hard and burnt out a connecting rod in the motor so he let the finance company repossess it. I purchased it from a car lot in Kamloops for about $200 as is where is. I put a short block in it and drove it until about 1963. Over the years when I was driving it I had it repainted about three times. It was then stored until the fall of 1997 when I brought it to Cranbrook and started work on restoring it. I think the top and upholstery were new when I first saw it in 1955. When I started restoring it, the original upholstery was underneath the existing material and was the same general type of material.

The information I have on the car is that there were 825,220 Chevrolets built in the U.S. in 1937 and 44,203 Canadian cars built. There were 1,724 U.S. cabriolets built and using the same averages it would mean that there were only 88 Canadian cabriolets built. My car is a Canadian-built cabriolet. The original selling price was $725 U.S.

I am enclosing a picture of the car taken in December 1956 and a recent picture after the restoration. I am driving it in the recent picture.

1937 CHEVROLET
Series 12-00 Master and 10-00 Master DeLuxe

Serials 12-00—7-12-01-00001 to 7-12-67-15902;
10-00—7-10-01-00001 to 7-10-87-09382.
Started Oct., 1936
(Located on right side of cowl under hood)

MOTOR—High compression, valve-in-head Six. Four main bearings. Five point rubber mountings. Light weight, slipper type pistons. Thermostatic carburetor heat control. Octane selector. Pressure-stream lubrication. DEVELOPS 85 horsepower at 3200 R.P.M. B. & S. 3½ x 3¾. N.A.C.C. 29.5. P. Disp. 216.5 cu. in.
WHEELBASE—112¼ inches.
OVERALL LENGTH—188 inches.
TIRES—6.00/16—pressure 28-28.
BRAKES—Hydraulic. Parking brake cable-controlled on rear wheels.
BODY—Fisher Unisteel Turret Top. No-draft ventilation. V-type windshield. Safety glass. Completely insulated against noise, heat and cold.
FEATURES—Knee-action front wheels and shockproof steering on 10-00 Series. Semi-elliptic springs and worm and sector steering on 12-00 Series. Box girder frame. Combined starter and accelerator pedal on 10-00 Series. Torque tube drive. Rear spring covers on 10-00 Series. Synero-mesh transmission.

PASS.	MODEL		WEIGHT	FACT. LIST	TOR. DEL.
5	Coach	12-01	2820	$ 695	$ 828
5	Coach, Trunk	12-11	2850	730	856
5	Sedan, Trunk	12-19	2900	805	936
2	Bus. Coupe	12-17	2760	680	803
2-4	Conv. Coupe	12-67	2820	910	1061
7	Sedan—127" W.B.	12-23	3300	1080	1243
5	Coach	10-01	2920	770	920
5	Coach, Trunk	10-11	2950	800	944
5	Sedan, Trunk	10-19	2970	885	1037
2	Bus. Coupe	10-17	2870	755	896
2-4	Sport Coupe, R.S.	10-87	2930	795	947

All Prices License Extra

"The Complete Car — Completely New"

(35)

Page 34 of the *1942 Used Car Sales Handbook of Features* (published by General Motors of Canada to help their salespeople sell used cars) lists Gordon Webb's 1937 Chevrolet convertible as a "2-4" passenger car because it has a rumble seat. The factory list price when new was $910 and could be "Toronto delivered" for $1061.

Loaded with Extras

THIS 1937 FORD SEDAN was photographed in 1939, perhaps near Dalrymple Lake (about twenty miles east of Orillia, Ontario). Harold Spence (first cousin of Ron Metcalfe's dad) owned the car and is seen here with his wife, Olive, and three-year-old Ron. Note the fender skirts, whitewalls, grille guard, and fog lights.

Side-opening Hood on 1937 Buick

THIS 1937 BUICK FOUR-DOOR sedan is getting a new fan belt at an Imperial Oil service station in Toronto in 1940. The man with his foot on the bumper is no doubt the car's owner. Note the Atlas carton he's holding and the fan belt being manoeuvred into position by the service attendant, who is no doubt thankful this car does not have the spare tires mounted in the front fenders, greatly restricting engine compartment access.

The hood consists of four folding panels, two on each side. Ford adopted the "alligator" hood in 1937. It opened from the front, and helped to set the trend for the vehicles of today.

"Alligator" Hood on 1937 Ford Coupe

YOUNG PETER RAMSAY IS WORKING on his hot-rodded '37 Ford coupe on the family farm near Stroud, Ontario, in the early 1950s. This was the first year for the "alligator" hood on Ford cars, replacing the older hoods that opened from each side. The '37 Ford was the first Ford with an all-steel roof, an idea introduced on GM cars two years earlier with their "turret top."

Bill's '37 Ford was powered by an original-style flathead V-8, but he had replaced the Ford transmission with a much stronger one from a late-1930s Cadillac-LaSalle. Now he could throw speed shifts with the gas pedal rammed to the floor. The muffler was non-existent. His dad, Art Ramsay (used car sales manager at Ontario Automobile, 1001 Bay Street in Toronto), told Peter to test-drive his car as far away from the house as possible on their fifty-acre property because of the noise, which rivalled the roar heard every summer evening from the stock car races at nearby Speedway Park.

Aunt Constance and Her 1938 Graham

THIS PHOTO OF RON MORGAN'S 1938 Graham super-charged sedan was taken when the car was nearly new and owned by Ron's Aunt Constance, seen here with her high leather riding boots and her dog, Dobie. She had the car repainted yellow (original colour was possibly green) around 1942, and that paint (except for black fenders) might still be on the car today. This photo was taken in front of the Blue Goose tourist cabins owned by Aunt Constance in Niagara Falls, Ontario.

This and other photos were given to Ron Morgan by his cousin Twila. She can vividly remember driving her aunt's super-charged Graham at ninety miles an hour along the Queen Elizabeth Way soon after it opened in 1939.

Ron Morgan's 1938 Graham

RON STANDS PROUDLY IN THE service bay of his Supertest gas station at Dixon and Islington in Toronto around 1959 with the '38 Graham super-charged sedan he acquired from his Aunt Constance. All 1938 Grahams were powered by an L-head six with 218 cubic inches. The optional super-charger boosted the horsepower from a modest 90 to a tire-squealing 116.

Ron Morgan was born in Toronto on Friday, October 17, 1930, just one year after the big stock market crash of 1929. The Morgans lived in the St. Clair–Oakwood area through the 1930s, at first on Glenholme and then on Alberta Avenue. The family often visited Ron's maternal grandmother in Smithville (in the Niagara Peninsula), and

Ron can vividly recall sitting on the big screened-in front porch on Sunday evenings and watching all the weekend traffic creeping bumper-to-bumper toward the S-curve on Highway 20. The QEW had not opened yet, and Ron was able to study all the slow-moving cars in detail. That is how he got to know all the makes: Hudsons, DeSotos, Studebakers, Hupmobiles, Reos, Whippets, Frontenacs, LaSalles, and of course, all the makes still being made today.

Meanwhile, back in Toronto, Ron moved with his family to Etobicoke in September of 1939, just after the outbreak of the Second World War. Here is where Ron's interest in cars really began to heat up. He vividly remembers the B-A gas station on the northeast corner of Bloor and Islington. It was a very old station dating back to the 1920s; it had a canopy over the pumps and was run by Walter Rand, who lived above the station.

Ron landed his first part-time job at that station when he was twelve years old. That was in 1942, and the gas came out of a pair of clear-vision "high boys," which could be pumped by hand when necessary.

Meanwhile, back on the farm … Ron had cousins at Wellandport who owned a Model T truck during the Second World War. It ran on purple tractor gas — and that gas occasionally went into their '39 Plymouth coupe. That's the car Ron used for his driver's test in 1946, just after turning sixteen. He went to nearby Beamsville for the test — and why not? The examiner was his cousin and the town had only one stoplight. Ron passed with flying colours.

Soon after getting his license, Ron became the proud owner of his first car: a 1930 Durant "614" four-door sedan. Ron's father gave it to him, and it had been in the family since the early 1930s. Ron drove it for two years, then got rid of it down Niagara way when the rear end gave out.

It was now 1948, and Ron's next car was a real beauty. It was a 1936 Nash sedan with 1937 front-end sheet metal (possibly the result of a previous accident). In any event the car came from British Columbia. Ron's dad bought it and then Ron bought it from his dad: five dollars a week for forty weeks (total price: two hundred dollars). The Nash had overdrive and was a real pleasure to drive and Ron drove it right into the early 1950s.

He landed his first full-time job in the gasoline business in October 1949 when he began working at the new Sunoco station on the south side of Bloor Street between the South Kingsway and Riverside Drive (2515 Bloor Street West, phone Murray 3556). It was operated by Bob Shill, and Ron worked there until he got a gas station of his own in 1957.

Ron, by this time, had traded in his '36 Nash for a new 1952 Prefect — but he found that car too small now that he was married with a growing family. He replaced the Prefect with a 1950 Ford sedan, followed somewhat later by a 1954 Pontiac sedan. Ron drove that Pontiac for five years, then sold it, then bought it back for thirty-five dollars.

In 1959 Ron began operating the Supertest gas station on the northeast corner of Dixon and Islington. Still driving the '54 Pontiac, he welded two vertical pipes to the front bumper, then wound a pair of battery cables around these and used the car as a service vehicle for booster calls. For towing cars into the station Ron used a Holmes wrecker on a '48 Ford truck.

The favourite car that Ron owned during his Supertest years was the 1938 Graham "Sharknose" super-charged sedan, originally purchased nearly new by Ron's Aunt Constance, who drove it for a number of years, then stored it in a barn near the village of Fenwick. That's where the squirrels got into it.

After Ron acquired the car he replaced all the brake lines and did all the body work. When the car was finished it was a very flashy yellow with black fenders. Ron drove it for a while, then sold it to a friend named Tom Keeling, who stored it in a garage on Lennox Avenue in downtown Toronto.

In the mid-1960s Ron left Supertest and operated a White Rose service station at Keele and Lawrence for a couple of years. Then in July 1966 he moved again, this time to the Shell service station at the Don Mills Centre, where he remained until his retirement in 1988.

In 1997, Ron Morgan phoned the man who had bought his super-charged Graham thirty years earlier. *He still owned it!* It was stored in a garage in downtown Toronto. Ron, along with "Old Car Detective" Bill Sherk, visited the Graham in storage and took lots of photos. The Graham has since been sold to a collector who is presumably restoring it.

Winter Snow and Slush, 1939

Looking south on Bay Street at Yorkville Avenue in midtown Toronto on Monday, February 27, 1939. The streets and sidewalks have been partially cleared following the last heavy snowfall. The Shell gas station on the left has a roof over the pumps. We can tell it's Shell by the shape of the sign. Further south on the same side you can buy a tankful of gas from Imperial Oil. Remember when nearly every corner had a gas station? Reo trucks are on sale on the other side of the street, named after the initials of Ransom Eli Olds, who started his automotive career by building Oldsmobiles over one hundred years ago. The 1933 or '34 Ford cabriolet speeding south through the slush may have already contracted a terminal case of rust-out from years of winter driving. No wonder so few have survived.

Vern Kipp

Prince Albert National Park, Saskatchewan, 1939

THE WOMAN TAKING THE PHOTOGRAPH is standing in the rumble seat of a 1936 Ford cabriolet on a beautiful summer's day along the shore of Waskesiu Lake in 1939 in Prince Albert National Park in northern Saskatchewan, "one of nature's playgrounds of western Canada."

This photograph was originally published in a 1939 calendar, and this particular photo appeared above August 1939 — the last month of peace before the outbreak of the Second World War.

Ford in 1936 offered Canadian buyers a total of fourteen different body styles, ranging from a business coupe to a convertible sedan.

National Archives of Canada, PA #68217

Checking Under the Hood

THE MAN IN THE FEDORA is watching the Esso service station attendant add water to the battery of his new 1939 Ford in Toronto. This was the first year that Ford Motor Company vehicles were equipped with hydraulic brakes — and the last year before virtually the entire auto industry adopted sealed-beam headlights in 1940. Note the small crank hole in the lower centre of the grille (in case your battery goes dead). This was a feature of Fords and Mercurys through 1948.

Advertisement in *LIFE* Magazine, June 5, 1939

Plymouth Introduces Power Top for Convertible, 1939

THE 1939 PLYMOUTH CONVERTIBLE COUPE represents a turning point in the evolution of the automobile. It was the last model year to offer a rumble seat (available only on Ford, Plymouth, and the Canadian Dodge in 1939) and the first year for a power-operated convertible top, also available that year on Lincoln-Zephyr convertibles (according to a report in the *Montreal Star*).

On the 1939 Plymouth convertible coupe (the four-door convertible top was still manual), the switch to operate the top was on the dashboard to the left of the instrument cluster, and was easily accessible by the left hand.

As an interesting variation, the 1940 Plymouth catalogue shows the power top control to be mounted at the far right of the dashboard and illustrates the driver reaching across with her right hand (many car companies aimed their power top ads at women). This unusual location was perhaps a safety feature to prevent the driver from putting the top up or down while the car was moving.

Toronto Star Photo Archives

War Hero Rides in 1939 Plymouth Convertible

FREDERICK GEORGE TOPHAM WAS BORN on Friday, August 17, 1917, in the family home on Beresford Avenue in Toronto's west end. After the outbreak of the Second World War, he enlisted and sailed for England as a member of the 1st Canadian Parachute Battalion.

Near the end of the war, he risked his own life several times in order to rescue injured soldiers and carry them to safety. When praised for his bravery, he refused to take any special credit for what he had done: "I only did what every last man in my outfit would have done."

He returned home to Toronto in the summer of 1945. On August 1, word came from London that Topham would be awarded the Victoria Cross. A victory parade in downtown Toronto was organized for August 10, and thousands turned out to cheer their newest hero, who rode in a 1939 Plymouth convertible.

129

Mayfair Magazine, April 1940

McLaughlin-Buick Convertible, 1940

MAYFAIR MAGAZINE FOR APRIL 1940 announced a new dimension in top-down motoring: "Four new convertible models — two coupes with special automotic tops and two Phaetons — have been added to the Series 50 and Series 70 line of 1940 McLaughlin-Buick cars. Illustrated above is the Series 70 Roadmaster convertible coupe which is acclaimed for its beauty of design, performance and comfort features. The front seat is five feet from door to door, while there is a full width seat in the back with greater luggage capacity built into the trim tail under the rear deck."

If you were buying a new Buick in 1940, you had five series from which to choose: Special, Super, Century, Roadmaster, and Limited. Prices in Canada ranged from $1374 for the 1940 Buick Special sport coupe all the way up to $3440 for the Series 90 Limited limousine (both prices factory retail, Oshawa). The Special, Century, and Limited employed face-lifted 1939 bodies. The Super (a new series for 1940) and Roadmaster employed the new streamlined bodies, which became the norm for 1941. When the new Super and Roadmaster for 1940 were introduced in the fall of 1939, they were available only as closed models — a six-passenger sport coupe or a six-passenger four-door sedan. No convertibles — at least not yet. The open models for Super and Roadmaster arrived in the spring of 1940, and they were available as convertible coupes and convertible sedans. The *Saturday Evening Post* for March 9, 1940, contained a lavishly illustrated two-page ad announcing these new convertibles for the 1940 Buick. These new open models were available in Canada as well as the United States, but they were beyond the reach of the average new car buyer in wartime Canada in 1940.

According to the *1942 Used Car Sales Handbook of Features*, published by General Motors of Canada, the Oshawa factory retail prices were: $1832 for a 1940 Buick Super convertible coupe (with automatic top), $2351 for a 1940 Buick Super four-door Phaeton convertible, $2170 for a 1940 Buick Roadmaster convertible coupe (automatic top), and $2687 for a 1940 Buick Roadmaster four-door Phaeton convertible.

Bathing Beauty on 1940 Mercury

VIOLET CHATTERSON IS THE BATHING beauty posing on the left front fender of this new 1940 Mercury on Wednesday, July 2, 1940. According to the notations in the *Globe and Mail* Collection at the City of Toronto Archives (where this photo was discovered), this lady was no shrinking violet. She supplied the newspaper with her address (27 Ascot Avenue, just north of St. Clair and Dufferin in Toronto) and even her phone number: Kenwood 1464.

Violet's left foot is resting on the front bumper, which has a ridge extending its full width to set it apart from its less expensive corpo-rate cousin, the 1940 Ford. Her right foot is resting on one of the two large accessory fog lights. Note the fancy grille guard bolted to the centre of the front bumper — a useful extra-cost item to protect the fifty-plus grille bars (made of white metal and easily broken).

Many new car buyers in wartime Canada in 1940 still chose black over a wide range of colours now available. The 1940 Mercury was launched in the fall of 1939 with eight colours to choose from: Mandarin Maroon, Yosemite Green, Lyon Blue, Como Blue Metallic, Sahara Tan, Cloud Mist, Folkestone Gray, and of course black. Three more colours were added in the spring of 1940, bringing the total to eleven.

The only black part of the '40 Mercury Violet is sitting on are the tires. Whitewalls would liven up the look of the car, but perhaps were deliberately not chosen in order not to distract the eye from Violet.

If this photo had been taken ten years later with a 1950 Mercury, Violet could have been wearing a bikini. That word first entered the English language in 1946:

On July 1, 1946 a Joint U.S. Army–Navy task force detonated an atomic bomb on Bikini Atoll in the Pacific. Four days later French fashion designer Louis Reard unveiled his latest creation at a Paris fashion show: a skimpy, two-piece bathing suit. The atomic explosion at Bikini and Reard's new bathing suit captured world attention almost simultaneously, and so Reard named his new brainchild the bikini. The first one was modeled by French designer Micheline Bernardi, whose explosively stunning figure was carried by newspapers around the world. She received fifty thousand fan letters.[16]

Jim Featherstone

Dick Riley's 1940 LaSalle Convertible

THIS BEAUTIFUL 1940 LaSALLE SERIES 50 convertible coupe was purchased new in Toronto by Dick Riley (right), a well-to-do bachelor and man about town who boarded for several years with a family at 156 Priscilla Avenue in the west end of the city. This photo was taken when the car was new, and the black-on-yellow 1940 Ontario plate is on the passenger side at the front. Over fifty years after it was taken, a member of the family where Riley boarded passed this photo along to Jim Featherstone, who passed it along to the author of this book.

The LaSalle was introduced by General Motors in March 1927 to fill the price gap between Buick and Cadillac, a decision in keep-ing with GM president Alfred Sloan's policy of offering "a car for every price and pocketbook." It was the policy that helped General Motors become the corporate giant it is today.

Named after the French explorer of the Mississippi River, the LaSalle offered Cadillac luxury at a bargain price (the Cadillac, incidentally, was named in 1902 after the French leader who founded Detroit in 1701). The stylish new LaSalle was born in GM's newly created Art and Colour Section (British spelling was used for an added touch of class), and the new car launched the young Harley Earl on his dazzling thirty-year career as the company's top designer.

By the end of the 1927 model year, the LaSalle accounted for 25 percent of the Cadillac division's total sales, and by 1929 LaSalle was outselling Cadillac 11 to 9. During the 1930s, LaSalle sales helped Cadillac stay afloat. In the grim Depression year of 1933, total division sales were a meagre 6,700 units, half of which were LaSalles. In 1937, combined sales were 46,000, with LaSalle accounting for 32,000 of those.

But the "bean counters" at GM were sharpening the axe. The recession of 1938 cut sales figures in half, and new styling for 1939 failed to produce the anticipated results (only 23,000 LaSalles of all body styles were built that year).

Although it is often difficult to prove why people buy a particular car, GM accountants kept insisting the LaSalle was pulling sales away from the more expensive (and more profitable) Cadillac. The LaSalle was dropped at the end of the 1940 model year, making Dick Riley's Series 50 convertible one of the last shining examples of this once-proud marque.

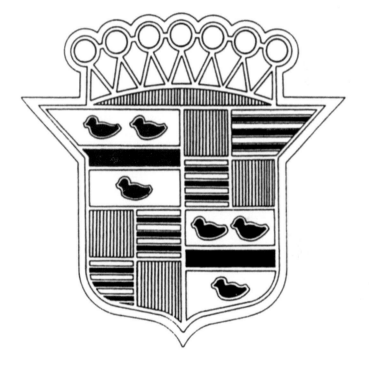

Mike Filey

Directing Traffic at Sunnyside, early 1940s

THIS POLICE OFFICER IS KEEPING the traffic moving along Lakeshore Boulevard in Toronto in the early 1940s. Sunnyside amusement park, with its roller coaster and red hots, was a popular gathering place for Torontonians from 1922 to 1955. When it was torn down to make way for the Gardiner Expressway, the merry-go-round was purchased by Walt Disney. It's still operating at Disneyland in Anaheim, California. And the cars? A 1940 Buick sedan, a 1939 Dodge sedan, a 1939 Mercury convertible ... If only we could go back in time and watch the traffic all day long!

Young Couple in 1939 Mercury Convertible, Quebec

THIS YOUNG COUPLE APPEARS JUST about ready to go for a spin in this 1939 Mercury convertible somewhere in Quebec in the early 1940s. The radio aerial tells us they can pull in all the currently popular songs as they breeze along with the breeze. They might even hum along as they listen to "Mares eat oats and does eat oats and little lambs eat ivy."

Calgary Service Station, circa 1941

BROCK SILVERSIDES WROTE: "ED AND Ted's staff filled your tank, checked fluid levels, cleaned the windshield and tested your brakes. If you couldn't make it under your own power, their '37 International wrecker would push or tow you in. Snappy looking white lettered coveralls on the pump jockeys is a classy touch seldom seen in today's serve yourself world."[17]

Bob Chapman's 1931 Chrysler Roadster, Toronto, 1941

BOB CHAPMAN WAS BORN ON Monday, January 8, 1923, in the front bedroom of the family home that still stands at 256 Gledhill Avenue in the east end of Toronto. At age seventeen, he was hired as a "ramper" at Ontario Automobile, a large Chrysler-Plymouth dealership at 1001 Bay Street in downtown Toronto. The year was 1940. Soon after starting work there, Bob found the car of his dreams.

"It was in the service garage at 1009 Bay Street and it was parked right beside a pillar. I can still see it to this day," he recalled.

It was love at first sight. He was looking at a 1931 Chrysler roadster with running boards, rumble seat, spoke wheels, fold-down windshield, Cord-like grille, and overall classic styling that made it look far more expensive than the two-hundred-dollar asking price.

But it wasn't available for purchase just yet. The owner had fallen behind in the payments and the car had been repossessed. But the law required that a repossessed car had to be held for twenty-one days before the dealer could resell it. This three-week grace period was designed to give the owner of the car an opportunity to catch up on car payments.

But Bob was able to start driving the car right away — even before he bought it.

Ontario Automobile stored its surplus cars and trucks in the terminal warehouse at the foot of York Street on Toronto's waterfront. The building is still there.

Bob drove many cars back and forth between the dealership and the warehouse — including that beautiful '31 Chrysler roadster, which had to remain in the warehouse for the next three weeks. He drove it around inside the warehouse nearly every day, hoping and praying the owner would default on the payments.

His prayers were answered. The owner lost the car and Bob bought it. The salesman who handled the deal was Art Ramsay. "It was the only car I ever bought on time in my life," recalled Bob. "My father had to sign for me through a finance company. All the kids were driving Model As in 1940. That's all we had. And, of course, they thought I had gone right out of my tree to spend two hundred bucks on a car. I was making only ten a week."

Although it was his dream car, Bob is the first to point out that his roadster was not a "cream puff." The blue paint had faded, the leather interior was not in the best of shape, the roof pads were stained, and the top was faded. The mileage showed a little over fifty thousand. "The oil pressure needle hardly moved at all on the idle," recalled Bob. "The body was good, but it needed tires and a bunch of other stuff."

To jazz up the car, Bob purchased a can of white tire paint at Canadian Tire and proceeded to give his car a set of whitewalls. The spare had to be painted as well because it was fully exposed at the rear of the car. The white soon yellowed — so the tires had to be repainted frequently. "I should have bought that paint by the gallon," said Bob.

Bob was still living at home with his parents in the house he was born in. When he entered the Armed Forces, he drove back and forth to Newmarket for his basic training — and, of course, the car he was still driving was his snazzy 1931 Chrysler roadster. Sometimes he picked up two solders hitchhiking back to Toronto and he would ask them to chip in a dollar apiece to help pay for the gas. One of them had to ride in the rumble seat.

Bob drove the car winter and summer, and the side curtains didn't do a very good job of protecting driver and passenger from the weather. "It snowed as much inside the car as outside," recalled Bob. His roadster did not have the luxury of windshield washers. You simply threw snow on the glass to clean it off. Bob did install a primitive electrical item glued to the windshield for defrosting, but you had to remember to turn it off or it would run down the battery.

Bob and his future bride, Katie, often double-dated in the roadster with Stan Gordon and his wife, Audrey. If Bob did the driving somewhere, they would switch so Stan could drive home, or vice versa.

Even with the top up, they could talk to one another because the flap holding the small glass rear window could be lifted up and fastened to special hooks inside the top.

Because his rumble seat passengers had no protection from the weather, Bob installed a hot water heater in the rumble seat (similar to the one under the dashboard). To do this, he scrounged some heater hose from Ontario Automobile (he had by this time been promoted from ramper to installer) and ran the hoses under the floorboards and into the rumble seat. Most of the heat quickly escaped into the air, but it was better than no heat at all. A blanket helped to trap some of it.

Finally, the day came when he was shipped overseas. He bid farewell to his loved ones and parked his '31 Chrysler roadster in the family garage, where it sat for the next three years while Bob served his country in its time of need.

Bob returned from overseas at the end of the war and once again climbed behind the wheel of his '31 Chrysler roadster. He and Katie were married on May 10, 1946, and set out for New York City on their honeymoon.

Just before the wedding, Bob parked his roadster at the house of his good friend Ven Hardie's brother-in-law, Peter, on Ossington Avenue. This was just a precaution so Bob's friends couldn't booby-trap the car as a prank. Lots of pranks were played on honeymoon cars back then — dead fish on the exhaust manifold, stones inside the hubcaps, and a potato up the tailpipe so the car wouldn't start.

Bob felt safe in taking the roadster on a long trip because by this time he had rebuilt the engine, and many other parts as well. The engine had babbited bearings, and Bob had it completely rebuilt. The roadster was his daily driver, winter and summer.

They crossed into New York State on the Ivy Lea Bridge and enjoyed a wonderful drive through the Adirondacks on their way to New York City for their honeymoon. The weather in early May of 1946 was cool, especially in the mountains of upstate New York. There were times when they had to drive with the top up, and very often Bob and Katie had to stuff Kleenex into the cracks in the side curtains to cut the draughts. Sometimes they drove with the top down and the side curtains in place.

They experienced no mechanical problems with the car on their honeymoon — not even one flat tire. Bob made a point of driving all day with the headlights on to avoid over-charging the battery, otherwise the battery would boil over.

Katie poses for the camera at the side of the highway as she and Bob drive through the Adirondacks on their honeymoon.

After the war, Bob and his friend Stan Gordon operated Blantyre Automotive, a repair shop and service station at Blantyre Avenue and Kingston Road in Toronto's east end. He had been driving the

Chrysler roadster for nearly ten years when he finally sold it. Here is how that happened:

I had the car repainted yellow with black fenders, and I kept it washed and parked out by the curb in front of our shop. Every day, a fellow got off the streetcar and dropped in, wanting to buy the roadster. This went on, it seemed, forever. Finally he wore me down. I said he could have it for $450 — and at that time, that was a mountain of money. I never dreamt I would get that much money for the car. And that was more than twice what I paid for it in 1940. He bought it. Then I bought a '39 Chev from a customer for fifty dollars. I had to go down to Brighton to pick it up. It had no brakes, so I fixed the brakes down there and drove it back. So now I had another car and four hundred dollars in my pocket.

I didn't realize at the time what a mistake it was to sell the roadster. I last saw the car at my garage in 1949. Some young kid had it and it was parked on my lot with no tires on it. Then one day it was gone. I'm sure it must have been scrapped.

As the years rolled by, Bob Chapman saw a lot of cars come and go — but he still cherished the memory of that wonderful '31 Chrysler roadster from the days of his youth. He never dreamed that someday he would own another one.

Then, one day in 1996, Bob's son Terry phoned to say he had spotted an ad in *Hemmings Motor News*. Someone in Cleveland, Ohio, was selling a 1931 Chrysler roadster.

Bob bought the car, pictured below, and brought it home. It's a real beauty! And when Bob and Katie go for a spin, they feel young all over again.

City of Toronto Archives, TTC Series 71, # 13716

Bus Service for War Workers

It's Monday, March 24, 1941, and Toronto buses are serving wartime workers at factories in Leaside (now part of Toronto). The side view of the Model A Ford coupe shows the fancy trim added to the louvers on the side of the hood. Note the fabric-insert roof on four of the six cars parked in the foreground.

Customized 1936 Ford Roadster, 1942

IN 1942, GORDON FAIRBANKS OF Montreal drove his radically customized 1936 Ford roadster to New York City. This photo was taken on Lennox Avenue in the heart of Harlem across the street from the Roseland Ballroom. The marquee reads: "Bob Allen Orchestra Fri. Sept. 4." This date pins down the year of the photo as 1942.

The Fairbanks roadster had several interesting features: a chopped top, a V-windshield from a '29 Auburn speedster, twin spotlights, a modified grille, twin fog lights, ribbed bumpers from a '37 DeSoto, a McCulloch super-charger, exhaust headers exiting through the hood side panels, custom paint scheme, removed running boards, and a Columbia two-speed rear axle.

Sometime after this photo was taken, the car reportedly won a prize at a car show in New Jersey. Its current whereabouts: unknown.

Alex Horen's 1932 Ford, Windsor, 1943

ALEX HOREN PURCHASED THIS '32 Ford V-8 four-door sedan from his brother Morris in November 1942 for $115. The car was ten years old but ran well and was in good shape. Morris fixed up cars damaged in accidents. The only part of this Ford in need of repair was the area around the left rear quarter window. Something had struck the car high up and dented this part of the body.

By the time this photo was taken on Drouillard Road in east Windsor in the early summer of 1942, the dent had been repaired but the cream pinstripe running along the beltline had not yet been reapplied around the quarter window.

The car was black with cream wheels, and Alex has many fond memories of his days and nights behind the wheel. One night around 2:00 a.m. he ran out of gas by a cemetery and had to walk home.

He's the one in the overcoat. His friend Julian had already enlisted. George is in the background, and Leo took the picture.

Alex, Julian, and Leo had travelled to California by hopping freights during the spring and summer of 1942. Alex's wife, Millie, is now completing a book (*He Never Said Good-bye*) chronicling their many adventures out west.

Alex Horen

Alex Horen's 1921 Gray-Dort Touring, circa 1958

ALEX HOREN GOT BITTEN BY the "old car bug" in the early 1950s — and he's been active in the old car hobby ever since:

In 1951 I was driving down Tecumseh Rd. in Windsor, Ont., when I spotted an old car on a used car lot near George Ave. I drove in there and I said to the salesman: "What the heck is that?" He said: "It's an old Chev." He had just sold a car to some people from Lambeth who drove the old Chev in. Fifty dollars was the price and I drove it home.

That old car was a 1917 Chevrolet "490" touring in original roadworthy condition. The "490" was named for its price when new and was designed to compete head-on with Henry Ford's very successful, low-priced Model T, which was selling for around five hundred dollars in 1917.

Alex didn't have the "490" for long. Albert Stedelbaur (Alex's boss at that time at Downtown Chev-Olds in Windsor) saw the "490" and said: "Alex, I'll give you five hundred dollars and a 1927 Chev four-door in beautiful shape." Stedelbaur ended up giving the "490" Chev a full restoration.

144

The most intriguing old car that Alex Horen has owned from the standpoint of low original mileage was the 1921 Gray-Dort touring he purchased in River Canard in 1952. He recalled:

I was working at Downtown Chev-Olds in Windsor at that time, when a guy came in and told me about an old car owned by an eccentric old timer in River Canard. So I went out there to have a look at it.

I came to the house — a wreck of a house with weeds five or six feet high all around it. I knocked on the back door and a tall fellow with a long beard came out. I said: "I understand you have an old car here. Would you like to sell it?"

He said: "Well, I'm not going to give it away." I went away without buying it, but I did find out it was a Gray-Dort. My wife and I were living with her parents at the time at their motel, and when I got home, I mentioned the car.

My father-in-law said: "A Gray-Dort! I used to own a Gray-Dort. We drove it out west."

So out of respect for this history, I went back and I bought the car for one hundred and thirty-five dollars. We had to tear the tar-paper off to get the garage doors open.

And was the car in good original condition? "Original?" recalled Alex. He went on:

I looked under the fenders. No mud. They were as shiny underneath as they were on top. I checked the seats. Like new. Then I checked the speedometer: three hundred and twenty-six miles. I asked the man if that was the real mileage. He said it was. He bought it new, then drove it a little, then put a five-dollar ding in the right rear fender when he hit a bridge. He never drove it again. The car was brand new.

Gray-Dort automobiles (a team effort between William Gray and Dallas Dort) were built in Chatham, Ontario. They came on the market in 1915 and sold well all across Canada into the early 1920s. Then the Dort car in Michigan ceased production in the mid-1920s. The major source of parts for the Gray-Dort was gone, and the car faded into history. The Zalev Brothers (scrap dealers in Windsor) demolished the Gray-Dort factory in 1937.

Alex drove his nearly new Gray-Dort for many years on various outings. It is now on display at the Transportation Museum at Heritage Village, about fifteen miles south of Windsor, Ontario.

The photo shows Alex in typical 1920s garb with his 1921 Gray-Dort in a park in Windsor around 1958. Alex was the first president of the Windsor Antique Automobile Club, which began in his living room in September 1954 with seven other old car enthusiasts. At that time, Alex said, "Some day this club will build a museum." The Transportation Museum at Heritage Village today is the realization of that dream.

Hauling Coal in a Rumble Seat, 1945

LET'S PAUSE FOR A MOMENT to recall the winters of long ago, when many homes in Canada were heated by coal. You could be dozing off in an easy chair with the evening paper at your feet, when suddenly you'd be awakened by a great rumbling noise from the basement. The coal truck driver was making another delivery by emptying several burlap bags full of coal into your coal storage bin. It would be up to you to shovel it into your furnace. No wonder people switched to oil or natural gas.

In the accompanying photo, we see bags of coal being loaded into the rumble seat of a 1933 or '34 Ford cabriolet (note roll-up window on driver's door). The three hinges visible on the rear edge of the door remind us that these cars had suicide doors.

When this photo was taken in 1945, the car was already over ten years old, and showing some signs of age. A crack appears to be forming on the upper centre of the rear fender wheel opening, and the convertible top appears to have been coated with some waterproofing.

The license plate is mounted above the left rear tail light, and the Ontario plate colours for 1945 were white on blue. Just beyond the tail light stem can be seen the gas filler cap.

Wire wheels on Ford cars would have one more year to go; they were replaced by steel rims with the advent of the 1936 models. The car in the photo would have mechanically operated four-wheel brakes unless the owner had updated the car by converting to hydraulic brakes, which first appeared on Ford Motor Company vehicles in 1939.

Is the Ford in the photo a 1933 or a '34? According to *The V-8 Album*, published by the early Ford V-8 Club of America, you could tell the two apart (aside from the slight difference in the grille) by the trim stripes around the body on the moulding just below the upper door hinge. The '33 had two stripes whereas the '34 had three with the centre stripe thicker than the other two. Unfortunately, the car in the photo has been repainted, and the trim stripes are gone.

Blonde Pushes Truck Uphill, 1945

THE WOMAN IN THE FUR coat certainly has the attention of the two men in the photo. The driver isn't even watching the road. Are these two guys in a hurry to get to the top of the hill? I doubt it.

With her left hand, the blonde is firmly clutching the bracket sticking out from the driver's side of the pickup bed. The other matching bracket can be seen on top of the front fender. This truck was obviously designed to carry long lengths of boards, pipes, eavestroughs, etc.

To the left of the blonde's left hand is some lettering too faint to read. But just below that are these words: "Supplies, 499 College Street, Toronto." A search through an old City of Toronto directory would reveal the name of the business that operated this truck. It's a Ford of 1932–34 vintage.

City of Toronto Archives, TTC series 71, #15336

Free Parking at King and Parliament, 1946

WE'RE LOOKING SOUTHWEST FROM KING and Parliament streets near downtown Toronto on Tuesday, April 9, 1946. The horse hitched to the Acme Farmers Dairy wagon soaks up the spring sunshine. The parked cars are sitting on property owned by the Toronto Transit Commission, from whose archives this photo is taken.

By this time, new cars were rolling off the assembly lines after a wartime shut-down of over three years (civilian production of automobiles had ended in February 1942). Some of the new 1946 models had wooden bumpers because of a shortage of steel.

Earl Domm considered himself lucky to be able to buy a new 1946 Hudson from Century Motors on Yonge Street, south of Bloor in Toronto. Not only did it have wooden bumpers, it also had no back seat and the plastic knob at the end of the gearshift lever was missing. All these parts were on back order. Meanwhile, in driving to the family cottage on Lake Simcoe, Earl's two children, Jimmy and Georgina, had to sit on fold-up chairs in the back seat.

Bill Sherk

Tractor Out to Pasture, 1946

IT'S JULY 1946 IN ONTARIO as these children play on an old tractor rusting away on Bill Johnson's two-hundred-acre farm near Waltonian Inn on the south shore of Lake Nipissing. Farmer Johnson and his family were pioneers who cleared this land and settled here in 1905. His nickname was "Buckshot Bill," and many of his poems were published in the *North Bay Nugget*. The little four-year-old fellow with hands on the steering wheel is Bill Sherk, author of this book.

These children and their families spent their summers in near- by cottages built by "Buckshot Bill" in the early 1940s. One was a log cabin, the other three were clapboard. All four cottages had an ice box, a wood stove, coal oil lamps, and an outhouse. There was no electricity and no indoor plumbing. The wood for the stove came from a wood pile beside each cottage. The blocks of ice for the ice box came from a nearby ice house where the blocks of ice were packed in sawdust. This ice was taken off the lake during the previ- ous winter. Each outhouse was a short walk from the cottage, and before you closed the door and sat down, you had to check for snakes. The cottages rented for fifteen dollars a week.

Trunk or Rumble Seat? 1946

Bill and Orma Dyson sit in what appears to be a rumble seat in the back of this 1937 or '38 Chevrolet coupe — but it's actually a trunk and they are improvising. The year is 1946 in Ontario (note white-on-black license plate). North American production of rumble seats ended in 1939, but this young couple is keeping the idea alive.

Their son, Jim Dyson, grew up to become an avid enthusiast of old cars. In spring 2003, his 1965 Ford Falcon convertible (in mint condition) was on display in the lobby of the Ford of Canada headquarters in Oakville, Ontario.

Jim Dyson

Danforth Used Car Alley, Toronto, 1946

GORD HAZLETT OF *OLD AUTOS* wrote:

If you were to walk the Danforth from Broadview to Victoria Park in the pre- and post-war days, there were maybe 40 car lots with about 1000 cars for sale, all hoping to put you behind the wheel. Some of the major car lots I remember were Stoney's, Ted Davies, Jack Leonard, Drayton, Ken-Clair, Thompsons, Archie Allen and the controversial Ted Williamson.

New car dealers were Hogan Pontiac-Buick, Jack Robertson Ford (later Chev-Olds), Giles Rice and Peters (Chev and Pontiac), Riverdale Garage (Ford),

Danforth Motor Car (Dodge), Watson Motors (Ford), Byers (Chrysler-Plymouth), and a Nash dealer I can't remember the name. Now I remember. It was Hamilton-Stiles.

Strings of light bulbs, tinsel streamers, flags, gaudy coloured pennants, flew from every car lot. Flashy salesmen stood out on the sidewalk to con you in. Radio jingles blared out to help get you in a buying mood. Some of the lots were paved but most were just cinders, some were 100-200 ft., others only 25 ft. frontage, some had a decent office, others a shack with a stove in it.

You could buy a used car, and some were really used, for a few dollars down and a buck or two a week. The cars we are now calling antiques could be bought for a song. That's why I can't come to grips to pay thousands of dollars for a Model T Ford I could have bought for $25.00.

Monday mornings were the best time to make a deal as, if there were many old cars sold on Saturday you may get a decent trade-in at a reasonable price. The salesman always told you the trade-in would be a lot more money after it was "reconditioned." This generally meant it was washed, a set of slipcovers installed (remember them?), the tires were re-grooved and painted until they looked like new, and maybe they'd clean and set plugs and points. No compulsory safety check or certification was necessary. It was buyer beware. Guarantees were practically non-existent although some of the bigger lots would treat you right. Stoney's was one that had a good name.

The cars were mostly lined up in rows. The front row was the cream-of-the-crop, middle row just average, the rear rows were the working man's specials or the mechanic's chances, just one tow away from the wreckers.

After saying that, I bought a '48 Chev sedan off Ted Davies' rear row one time and it was one of the best cars I ever owned. I bought it on a Monday morning and it had been a Saturday trade-in deal from a farmer. It had a year's dirt on it and in it and looked terrible but that farmer never abused it mechanically.

It was the first car I ever owned with a cigar lighter, and the first time I used it (I foolishly smoked in those days), I lit my cigar and threw the lighter out the window. I thought I was using a match and had to retrieve it from the road. The back seat of this car I don't think was ever sat in by a human being but I believe there may have been the odd calf, pig, or bag of turnips hauled in the back seat.

Now the used car business on the Danforth is dead. Only five used car lots remain, plus eight lots east of Victoria Park. But nothing like the old heydays. Toronto will never be the same.[18]

Spinning its Tires on Avenue Road Hill, 1947

HEAVY SNOW FELL ON TORONTO on Wednesday, January 29, 1947, creating hazardous driving conditions all over the city. A particularly difficult spot for motorists was the big hill on Avenue Road a few blocks south of St. Clair Avenue. If you were heading south, down the hill, you ran the risk of sliding sideways until your car slammed into something. If you were heading north, up the hill, you had to build up enough speed to make it to the top. The car in the photo began spinning its wheels near the top of the hill, blocking the path of the streetcar coming up behind. The motorman (the driver of the street car) and another helper are trying to push the car over the top. Someone happened to be there with a camera, and this photo was published in the *Globe and Mail* the following morning.

The car is a Mercury 114, built by Ford of Canada from 1946 to 1948. Named for its 114-inch wheelbase, the Mercury 114 was built only in Canada and gave Mercury-Lincoln dealers across the country a car they could sell in the low-price field. The Mercury 114 shared its wheelbase with Ford and really was a Ford with Mercury trim and a slightly modified Mercury grille adapted to the Ford front fenders. The Mercury 114 cost approximately twenty-six dollars more than its Ford counterpart, and gave its owner the right to proudly proclaim: "I'm driving a Mercury."

The Mercury (named by Edsel Ford, Henry's only son) was first introduced in the fall of 1938 as a 1939 model, and was designed to help fill the price gap between the Ford Deluxe and the Lincoln-Zephyr. From the very beginning, the name Mercury was synonymous with medium-priced cars.

The American-built Mercurys from 1946 to 1948 rode on a 118-inch wheelbase and were sold in the United States as Mercurys. In Canada, they were marketed as the Mercury 118 to distinguish them from the 114. For the 1949 model year, Ford of Canada dropped the Mercury 114 and replaced it with another made-only-in-Canada car: the new 1949 Meteor.

"We've Been Everywhere!"

Rimouski … Riviere-du-loup … Quebec [City] … Montmagny … St. Anne de Beaupre. These two women proudly display the pennants from all the places they visited in la Belle Province. And judging by the luggage on the roof, they're not home yet. Note the 1948 Quebec license plate. The car is a made-only-in-Canada Mercury 114 (the 118 had different trim on the trunk lid). We can also say this car is the standard 114 and not the deluxe version (known as the 114X). That model had stainless trim around the windows. This one has plain black rubber.

The Mercury 114 sold well in Canada during its three-year production in 1946, 1947, and 1948. Over ten thousand were sold.

Wash This Car!

THIS MERCURY COUPE WAS PHOTOGRAPHED somewhere in Quebec when the car was relatively new. The woman with the sunglasses and ankle socks doesn't seem to mind having her picture taken alongside a car that's dusty and dirty from bumper to bumper — perhaps because many cars back then (especially in rural areas with no paved roads) looked like this all the time.

Movie companies rent vintage vehicles whenever a script calls for them. Often these vehicles are owned by collectors who have restored their pride and joy to showroom condition — and that's the problem. The cars look too good and too new. Most motorists fifty years ago were not driving new cars and often didn't have the

time (or even the inclination) to wash their cars whenever they got dirty. The author has attended movie shoots where the film crew sprayed dust all over shiny, restored cars to make them look more authentic.

Incident in a Small Town, starring Walter Matthau, was filmed in Beeton, Ontario, in 1993 and was set in a town in Illinois in 1954. When Jack Morton arrived with Vern Kipp's immaculate Maywood Green Metallic 1950 Mercury Sport Coupe, the film crew gave it a going-over that made it look as if it had just been driven ten miles over a dry and dusty dirt road.

The car in the photo is a mid-1947 or '48 Mercury 118, so

named for its 118-inch wheelbase. The 1946 Mercury 118s and the early 1947 models had grille frames painted to match the body colour, and also had stainless side trim extending almost to the front of the hood.

The outside sun visor was a popular accessory fifty or more years ago, and it helped to keep the interior a little cooler on hot summer days. These cars did not have air conditioning.

Sitting on a 1947 or '48 Buick

OLD CARS WERE GREAT FOR sitting on and having your picture taken because you could nestle your rump between the hood and front fenders. This Buick with Quebec plates was powered by Buick's legendary straight eight overhead-valve engine, in production from 1931 to 1953. Note the two-tone paint job on this Buick and how the darker colour comes down the centre of the hood and wraps itself around the grille. Note also the "gunsight" hood ornament and the rotating radio aerial above the windshield.

This Buick could be a 1947 or '48. Demand for new cars was so great after the war that GM kept these Buicks rolling off the assembly line with virtually no difference between the two model years.

Jim Watson

New 1949 Monarch, Leamington

MANLEY WATSON OPENED A SHOE store on Talbot Street East in Leamington in 1932. Seventeen years later, he purchased this beautiful cream and blue 1949 Monarch four-door sedan from Eaton Motors, just down the street from his shoe store. This photo was taken at the family home on Erie Street South with Manley and his son Jim, who operated the store after Dad retired. Jim's son, Scott, also worked in the store. Watson's Shoe Store served the Leamington community for over sixty years, up until Jim retired in the 1990s.

The Monarch was first introduced by Ford of Canada for the 1946 model year, and the name capitalized on the feelings of patri-

otism in Canada that attended the Allied victory in the Second World War. Those first Monarchs shared the same body and wheelbase as the Mercury 118, and gave Ford dealers a car to sell in the medium-priced field.

The 1949 Monarch pictured here was a Canadian version of the 1949 Mercury, which was also built and sold in Canada. But the Monarch was unique in being built and sold only in Canada, its name reflecting the close ties between Canadians and the royal family.

Bill Ramsay

"Step-down" Hudson, Novar, 1949

AT AGE SEVENTEEN IN 1949, Bill Ramsay of Toronto landed a summer job with a Hudson and Hillman dealer in the small town of Novar, Ontario (on Highway 11 between Huntsville and Burk's Falls). The dealer owned his own plane, and Bill sometimes flew with him back to Toronto on weekends.

Bill snapped this photo of a new 1949 Hudson parked alongside the Novar dealership. These "step-down" Hudsons were a radical departure in styling from all earlier Hudsons. They were first unveiled in October 1947 as '48 models, and were among the first new postwar designs on the North American market. They earned their "step-down" name because the floor was placed down in between the side rails of the unitized body instead of on them. This design lowered the height of the car dramatically. These Hudsons were powered by the biggest six-cylinders on the market, and they sold well until the early 1950s, when declining sales forced a merger with Nash to create American Motors Corporation on May 1, 1954.

Calder Hawkesford

Saskatchewan Youth Buys First Car

CALDER HAWKESFORD OF FILLMORE, SASKATCHEWAN, wrote:

When I was in grade twelve, I persuaded my parents that I really needed a car, and because of my newly-acquired part-time job, I could purchase such a beast, but I had to find one that was in decent shape.

The result was that, after much looking, I purchased a 1953 Morris Oxford sedan (you know one of those !@$% little English cars??) for the princely sum of $250.00. The Morris was not really my idea of "cool" transportation (I would much rather have

had a Ford or a Chev), but dad reminded me that the car was in rather good shape. It was shiny jet-black in colour, had four cylinders and a four-speed manual shift on the column, if you please. The real leather upholstery smelled luxuriously on that warm fall day when I went to pick it up, having bought it a couple of days before.

The two fellows who had previously owned the car had done a lot of work on it before selling it to me. First, they had "cobbled" together a continental kit and placed it on the trunk and rear bumper (extended about 8" from normal). It sounds dreadful, but it actually didn't look all that badly. The front fender chrome strips from a 1952 (or so) Mercury half-ton had been scrounged and placed on the front fenders of my car. These strips didn't look too out of place, but Ford Motor Company just had to put "Mercury" on them in great, huge, red letters. At traffic lights, when I later went "cruising," these "additions" made for some interesting comments from fellow motorists. They said really kind things such as, "Morris Mercury. Where the hell did you find that — the bottom of Wascana Creek??" or "Didja make that continental kid outa your Meccano set??" or "Hey hotshot, wanna drag??"

Anyway, I was now a proud member of the motoring public. That darn Morris carried my friends and me all over the place. I recall that on Saturday afternoons, six of us used to pile into it and travel to shoot pool in Pense, a nearby village. Being prudent with our money, we felt that shooting pool in Regina was simply too expensive — about 50 cents! I can remember how that Morris used to behave when it was fully loaded — with six guys in the car, I couldn't get more than 35 miles per hour out of it, wide open. The springs were fully pressed down; it's a wonder that we didn't drag bottom. We used that car every Saturday afternoon for about ten months, no matter how ridiculous we looked, or how bad the weather. Every so often, the filter of the SU electric fuel pump would clog and the car would conk out because it wasn't

getting fuel. I would swear profusely, get out, open the hood, tap the fuel pump with a pair of pliers, get the gas flowing again, start her up and continue our trip. Needless to say, the guys ribbed me unmercifully for buying such a piece of !#$%@. It took me the longest time to determine that the little black knob on the front of the fuel pump would actually give me access to the filter, and that with a little wind power, I could blow out all the dirt and sediment. I could then proceed for many miles with little or no problems.

I kept my Morris for a year and a half, eventually selling it through the newspaper. After advertising for about 10 years (or so it seemed), a "victim" phoned and actually wanted to come over to see it. He did and we agreed on a price: $190.00 (a $60.00 loss just to get rid of it!). After he made out his cheque, I asked him what he planned to do with the car. He replied that he wanted to take it to Prince Albert for his father. When I began to laugh, the new owner asked me whether I thought the car would travel that far. I said, "Of course it will. Just let me tell you about the fuel pump filter …"

I never saw the man or the car again. Some late winter nights when the wind is blowing and it's forty below outside, I think morbid thoughts. I wonder, then, just where that old Morris ended its days; whether or not it actually made it to Prince Albert. Poor devil that bought it — probably froze to death on Number Six Highway with a fuel pump filter in his hand.[19]

1949 Triumph 2000 Roadster, Toronto, 1956

THE RUMBLE SEAT ERA ENDED in North America in 1939 with only Ford and Plymouth and the Canadian Dodge offering this open-air seating, and only in their convertible models. But you could buy a new car with a rumble seat in Canada after the Second World War if you chose the Triumph 1800 roadster from 1946 to 1948, followed by the Triumph 2000 in 1949 (the numbers indicating the engine displacement in cubic centimetres). To protect rumble seat passengers from the wind, a little flip-up windshield was provided. Because of the low windshield, these cars were equipped with three windshield wipers instead of the usual two. Each wiper had a separate knob on the dash with a rod or cable connecting it to its wiper. And as each wiper swept the windshield, you could see each knob on the dash turning back and forth as well.

Gord Duncan

Jim Featherstone's 1941 Plymouth

Jim Featherstone and his good friend Brian Brady bought and sold (always at a profit) a total of fifteen 1940 Mercury convertible coupes in Toronto between 1948 and 1950. During that same time period, these two fellows also found time to purchase three previously owned Plymouth convertibles. Jim owned a light gray 1940 and a maroon '41, and Brian owned a yellow '41. This is the story of Jim's maroon '41.

He first saw the car at Ontario Automobile, the big Chrysler-Plymouth dealership at 1001 Bay Street in midtown Toronto. Jim lived nearby and often dropped in and walked around through the building. He knew several staff people by name.

One day, up on the second or third floor, he saw a 1941 Plymouth convertible in the final stages of being rebuilt. It had just been given a beautiful new maroon repaint job — which was an odd contrast to the blue leather interior, leading Jim to suspect maroon was not the original colour.

It had no running boards (they were an option in 1941) and the chrome wind wings on either side of the windshield were missing, with the holes filled in.

A few weeks or months later, Jim saw an ad in the *Toronto Daily Star* for a 1941 Plymouth convertible. The car was not available for viewing, and if you wanted to buy it, you had to mail in a bid.

Jim mailed in a bid of $1000 and it was accepted. A husband was selling it on his wife's behalf (they had lived in Port Hope, Ontario), and he was a member of the famous Massey family. He delivered it to Jim's place of work at Duke and George Streets (now Adelaide East and George). As soon as he saw it, Jim realized it was the same 1941 Plymouth convertible he had seen earlier being rebuilt at Ontario Automobile.

By the time Jim bought the car, the recent maroon repaint job had faded. Jim rolled up his sleeves and polished it to a dazzling gleam. Two days later, it faded again. It was a very good car, and Jim drove it through a good part of 1950 before selling it off to Barreca Motors.

Janet Reder on 1941 Dodge

WHEN YOU'RE SEVEN YEARS OLD in 1950, it's hard to find a better place to have your picture taken than on the front fender of Dad's 1941 Dodge. Janet Reder's parents, Jake and Elsie, moved from Leamington, Ontario, where this photo was taken, to Bayfield on Lake Huron a year or two later, where Jake served as a civilian driver at the RCAF base in nearby Clinton. He is now a retired vegetable farmer.

Janet married Murray McEwan, and they, along with Murray and Joyce Cutler, publish *Old Autos*, a twice-monthly newspaper for hobbyists. It began in 1987 with only a handful of subscribers. It now goes to over twenty thousand households all across Canada with an estimated readership of forty thousand people. For more information, call 1-800-461-3457 or visit their website at www.oldautos.ca.

Not the Better Way, 1952

ACCORDING TO THE CLOCK ACROSS the street, it's twenty to five. This is the afternoon rush hour on Queen near Mutual Street on Friday, January 18, 1952, in the middle of a Toronto transit strike that lasted three weeks. See if you can spot the bullet-nose Studebaker, a 1951 Meteor, a '51 Mercury, a Meteor with a sun visor, an Austin with a sun roof, and a '49 Ford with whitewall tires.

All the license plates on these cars are carry-overs from 1951 because of the Korean War metal shortage. Ontario plates for 1952 consisted of a yellow sticker on the windshield — and the Chrysler or DeSoto heading off-camera appears to have one.

Ed Janzen

Manitoba Adventures with a 1938 Plymouth, 1952

ED JANZEN OF BELWOOD, ONTARIO, wrote:

Mr. Wiens and his mechanics agreed that the 250 JAWA motorcycle wouldn't run right for me. They strongly encouraged me to buy the 1938 Plymouth 4-door sedan they had in the yard. I really didn't plan to have a car and I certainly didn't have any money. Mr. Wiens wanted $300 (my wife thinks it was $400) and he said I could pay him monthly once I was back in my teaching job. I drove the car home. It seemed to run fine.

Every morning my dad and I drove into Winnipeg for our summer jobs in my "new" '38

Plymouth. It had good road-holding ability and I was getting rather attached. This was 1952 and the car was already fourteen years old. However, it was my first car and I was quite proud to own it.

But one morning there was suddenly a loud knocking sound from the engine and lots of vapour coming from the motor. I stopped to check the radiator but everything seemed OK. So we took it a little slower and brought it into Mr. Wiens. He said I had a broken piston ring and that the motor would have to be overhauled.

He knew I didn't have any money so he allowed as how I could do most of the work myself. This sounded good to me since I was interested in learning something about mechanical things anyway. Mr. Wiens told me to get started by taking everything off the motor: carburetor, spark plugs, wires, generator, coil, etc. He wanted everything off the flat-head so I could get the head bolts off.

Some nuts just would not come off. As I applied more and more pressure, I torqued off one of the bolts. Patiently, Mr. Wiens showed me how to drill out the old bolt, thread the hole with a slightly larger bore, and put in a slightly larger bolt. Then the cylinders had to be bored and honed since the broken ring had left a scratch on the cylinder wall. Up and down, up and down, turning the crank by hand. No electrical power tools then. Mr. Wiens had me go much longer than I would

Ed Janzen

have by myself. I was getting sick of this boring stuff (sorry for the pun!). Eventually he gave in, but I don't think he really thought it was good enough. He had the mechanic assemble the engine and torque down the head bolts. I learned that this had to be done in a certain order. Each nut was finally tightened down with a torque wrench.

The '38 Plymouth now seemed to run real well. My girlfriend and I went all over. Mostly we were running errands to keep up with our mothers who were preparing for our wedding. Since my parents didn't have a phone and my girlfriend's farm was "long distance" it took a lot of driving but the Plymouth liked it.

[Ready for the wedding?] I had forgotten the ring in my suitcase at my grandparents' place. There was just enough time to go back and get it. My best man and friends didn't think so, and said we could fake it. But I would have nothing of this. And I certainly wanted the challenge of driving my '38 Plymouth out to North Kildonan and back in record time.

Off I went. I selected the Salter Bridge route, thinking that North Main would be too slow with traffic lights. The Plymouth went most of the way in second gear at high r.p.m. (which I paid for later). It was a wonderful run. Fast and devious. Luckily, no accidents. I ran no red lights and I saw no policemen (or no policemen saw me). I was back at the church on William and Juno just as the organ started and we were supposed to walk in. You will forgive the big smile on my face. The best man smiled too.[20]

Previous page: Ed Janzen with his '38 Plymouth during a Manitoba winter. Note the cover over grille and the extra pane of glass on the windshield.

Left: Ed's wife, Susan, relaxes in the front seat of their Plymouth in the summer.

1928 Chevrolet Roadster, Carlisle, 1953

KEITH ROBINSON OF MOUNT ALBERT, Ontario, wrote:

I attended the Niagara Parks Commission School of Horticulture in Niagara Falls from 1952 to 1955. A fellow student in third year owned a '28 Chev roadster. He had bought it from a fellow student, Jake Clark. Jake had bought it from an old man on McLeod Avenue in Niagara Falls. This man had purchased it new and had driven it a few times to Florida in the early days.

I bought the Chev in March 1953 for nineteen dollars. I drove it from spring to fall for my three years there and many times from Niagara Falls to my parents' home in Carlisle [Ontario].

In February 1953 (before I bought the car), I borrowed it for a date. It was a miserable night with rain and icy roads. I went to pick the girl up who lived in a very rich part of the city. I was invited into the house for a coffee and delayed leaving, not wanting her to see what she would be riding in. The car had a home-made top. The passenger door was wired shut and there was no upholstery on the seats, just a blanket over the springs. She had on a very expensive fur coat — and when she saw the car, she gasped.

We drove down Victoria Avenue and on coming to the intersection with Valley Way, the light was green but some cars were still stopped. I went around them as I couldn't stop. Before we got to the intersection the light turned red and a new '52 Ford went through on Valley Way. I hit him on the rear fender. The man and woman got out in a rage and he started chasing me around the cars, but being younger I could out-run him. He kept falling on the ice. Finally the police came and shut him up. I could tell they knew him (a mafia sort who later went missing).

It was agreed I would pay for repairs at the Ford dealer, Victoria Motors. The girl with me stood in freezing rain all this time with her fur coat covered with ice. She refused to get back into the car so we walked to a show. She didn't speak the rest of the evening.

She also refused to get into the car after the show so we took a bus and I walked her home (about four blocks).

When I got back to the bus stop, the last bus had gone so I walked about two miles to the car, which I had backed into a service station lot. It wouldn't start so I had to use the crank. I went to drive off but I couldn't steer. When I hit the other car it had pushed the bumper into the wheel. All I had to pry it out with was the crank, and each time I pried the bumper out, it would spring back. After a lot of work I finally got it far enough out to drive. I arrived back at the school about 3 a.m., cold, wet, and fed up. Needless to say, I never saw that girl again.

After graduation, Keith Robinson moved to Kingston and worked for the Department of Highways. He took the Chev there with him. In 1965 he was transferred to Toronto and stored his '28 Chev in a barn on Bathurst Street near Aurora. By spring it was gone (i.e. stolen). All he has left is the spare tire.

1953 Chevrolet Convertible, Kingsville, 1954

IN 1953, KEN HOPE OF Leamington, Ontario, began his thirty-six-year career with the H.J. Heinz Company near the south end of town. To get to work each day, he either walked or drove his 1948 Plymouth coupe down Erie Street, right past Wigle Motors, the local Chevrolet-Oldsmobile dealership in Leamington since 1923. One day, while going by, Ken spotted a new 1953 Chevrolet convertible parked at the front of Wigle Motors. It was powder blue with a dark blue top, dark blue inserts on the rear fenders, and a blue leather interior. Ken saw it there every day — and finally, in the fall of 1953, he bought it.

The sticker price was $3300, and that included the radio, heater, fender skirts, whitewall tires, and power top. It was the top-of-the-line Bel Air, and under the hood was a 235-cubic-inch, overhead-valve, six-cylinder engine with aluminum pistons. The transmission was a manual three-speed with column shift.

Ralph "Pete" Gulliver was the salesman who sold the convertible to Ken ("Pete" later opened his own GM dealership in nearby Wheatley — Gulliver Motors).

When all the papers were signed, "Pete" handed the keys to Ken, who drove away with the top down and the wind in his hair. He owned the car for ten years.

He was driving north one day on the Leamington Side Road (now Highway 77) with a carload of friends. The top was up.

Suddenly the top separated from the windshield and billowed up like a balloon, much to the shock of Ken and his passengers, who all shouted "Whoa!" By the time he stopped the car at the side of the road, the top was sticking straight up. It turns out Ken had forgotten to fasten the top to the windshield the last time he had put it up. The fabric didn't rip, but the arms connected to the power mechanism were now slightly bent. From then on, whenever he raised or lowered the top, it would get stuck halfway and he would have to give it a little push to keep it going.

In the summer of 1954, Ken drove his convertible to Saskatchewan, accompanied by two Leamington friends, Vic Harward and Lee Malott. The car ran fine out there and back.

After driving his convertible for ten years, Ken decided to sell it. The car still ran well, and aside from replacing the timing chain, he enjoyed trouble-free motoring all those years. But rust was taking its toll, and Ken sold the car to a local resident named Grieve. It finally rusted out completely and ended up at Quick's Auto Wreckers on the Albuna Town Line.

Thorncrest Ford-Monarch Dealership, Toronto, 1953

ON A RECENT TRIP NORTH of Oakville, Ontario, Kent Weale and I visited two veteran hot rodders: Bill Balzer and Bob Downey. Bill and Bob grew up in the west end of Toronto in the 1950s, and they owned and drove an amazing number of hot rods and customized cars back in the days of ponytails and blue suede shoes.

In preparing for our visit, I brought along an eight-by-ten photo of Dundas Street west of Islington Avenue, taken in June 1953. The photographer was J.V. Salmon, who took photos all over Toronto in the 1940s and 1950s. A collection of his photos can now be seen at the Toronto Reference Library at 789 Yonge Street. Bill

and Bob had grown up in the area where the photo was taken, and I knew they would enjoy looking at it.

The car in front of the showroom is a 1951 Meteor convertible, and the driver (wearing sunglasses) is waiting for traffic to pass so he can pull out and drive away.

When I showed the photo to Bill and Bob, I never could have imagined what happened next. Bob Downey took one look at the photo and exclaimed, "That's me! And that's my car!"

Bob Downey had turned sixteen in May 1953, and by the time the photo was taken one month later, he had purchased a fire-engine red 1951 Meteor convertible and was roaring around town with the top down.

He was able to positively identify the convertible in the photo as belonging to him. A close look at the front end shows the passenger side of the grille to be slightly higher than the driver's side. That's the way it was when Bob purchased the car from a young Italian fellow in the Bloor-Dufferin area shortly before this photo was taken. The fellow selling the car told Bob a truck had rolled back into the car (probably on a hill), and had slightly pushed up one side of the grille. The truck driver got out, apologized, gave the fellow twenty dollars to settle the matter, and drove off. Some time after this photo was taken, Bob replaced the grille with a new one.

By the end of the 1950s, Bob Downey had owned two 1951 Meteor convertibles, a 1937 Ford convertible with rumble seat, a radically channelled 1934 Ford three-window coupe, and a radically customized 1956 Meteor convertible.

Bob Downey's 1956 Meteor Convertible

BOB DOWNEY WAS A HOT rodder and custom car enthusiast who grew up in the west end of Toronto in the 1950s. One of his first cars was a 1951 Meteor convertible purchased from a pilot. He and his friends drove it to Buffalo one night — and on their drive back to Toronto, the original top fabric began to disintegrate. His friends helped this along by ripping pieces off as they drove along the QEW. He replaced the top with a new one and gave the car a nice "repaint job."

His most distinctive car was a 1956 Meteor convertible purchased from a dealership near Bloor and Islington in the west end of Toronto when the car was only about one year old. The dealer-installed clear plastic slipcovers were still protecting the light and dark blue interior seats.

The first photo shows Bob behind the wheel when the car was still in original condition. The '56 Meteor grille is especially attractive and has been used by American customizers to modify the front end of '55 and '56 Fords.

By around 1960, Bob had extensively customized his '56 Meteor in the custom styling trends of that time. A custom grille was flanked by canted quad headlights while the rear fenders were extended to flank a continental kit. The original tail lights were replaced with 1958 Edsel station wagon tail lights.

The second photo was taken at the Fort York Armoury Autorama in Toronto in the early 1960s. The small rear window on the convertible top was another custom touch that made this car an eye-catcher.

At the end of one of these car shows back then, Bob was driving his Meteor across the floor to the exit when he accidentally ran over a spray can of red paint left behind by another exhibitor. The can burst and red paint was splattered along the side of Bob's show car. He said: "That's it! I'm never putting my car in a show again."

And he never did. He put the car in storage and there it stayed as the years rolled by — many, many years. The author had the good fortune to see this car in the late 1990s when Bob Downey was still alive and the car was stored at the home of his friend, Bill Balzer, near Hornby, Ontario. The '56 Meteor was still in show car condition, and the seats were still covered in the original clear plastic slipcovers. Bob Downey passed away a couple of years later and gave the car to Bill Balzer.

Bob Brown

Bob Chapman

Ontario Automobile Dealership, Toronto, 1953

THIS COMPOSITE PHOTO COVERS BOTH sides of Bay Street in downtown Toronto in 1953. The new car showroom for Ontario Automobile was on the east side at 1001 Bay Street while the used car lot was on the west. Most of the used cars for sale are Chrysler products, but if you look closely, you'll see a Ford, a Mercury, a Prefect — and even a Kaiser!

Bob Chapman was hired as a "ramper" at this dealership in 1940. He was seventeen at the time. Rampers brought customers'

179

cars from the roof down to whatever level they were repaired on, then back up the ramps to the roof to wait for the customers to pick them up.

Bob (along with some other employees) was given an interesting assignment in 1942, just before he enlisted and went overseas. Civilian production of cars had stopped in February 1942 because of the war, and Ontario Automobile (a distributor for other dealerships) stored over fifty new cars in a large arena in Willowdale (at the north end of Toronto). Bob remembers parking them "door handle to door handle" and blocking the clutch pedal. These cars were set aside for essential service (doctors, armed forces, etc.) and were expected to last for the duration of the war.

After Bob went overseas, a heavy snowfall in Toronto caused the arena roof to collapse, damaging many of these cars. Bob's dad sent him the news clipping to keep him up-to-date on happenings back home. Bob carried that clipping in his haversack all over Europe, and brought it home when the war ended. He still has it.

Bob James

1947 Ford Sportsman, Quebec, 1954

IN MARCH 1954, BOB JAMES got a phone call from his dad, telling him to rush right over to Hart Motors, a Mercury-Lincoln-Meteor dealer where Bob's dad worked (just a short drive from Dorval Airport). A car had just been traded in on a new Mercury. The trade-in was a 1947 Ford convertible.

And what a convertible! It was a very rare wood-bodied 1947 Ford Sportsman for sale for $700. Bob took one look at it and bought it, using his '41 Ford rag-top as a trade-in. For the next two and a half years, Bob drove one of the rarest cars in all of Canada.

The Sportsman was a cross between a wood-bodied station wagon and a convertible, and was designed to generate excitement in Ford dealer showrooms as civilian automobile production resumed after the end of the Second World War. The first

Sportsman was delivered to Hollywood actress Ella Raines on Christmas Day in 1945, although general production did not begin until July 1946. The last Sportsman was built in November of 1947, and the last few were registered as 1948 models.

Bob still has the original bill of sale for his 1947 Ford when he purchased it on March 24, 1954, from Hart Motors Ltd. at 6458 Cote de Liesse Road in Dorval, Quebec. Bob's car is described as follows: "One only 1947 Ford — T & C Convertible — Green."

The letters "T&C" are a mistaken reference to the wood-bodied Chrysler Town and Country convertible on the new car market at the same time as the Ford Sportsman.

The bill of sale also indicates that Bob managed to get the $700 asking price reduced to $600, from which was subtracted $275 —

the trade-in allowance on Bob's 1941 Ford convertible. Bob had to pay the difference of $325 plus 2 percent provincial sales tax, bringing the total to $331.50. Also on the bill of sale is the serial number of Bob's Sportsman: #2061456.

A look at the other papers in Bob's Ford file reveals more interesting details. The tire guarantee that came with the car provides the name and address of the previous owner: R.G. Villeneuve at 3499 Delormier in Montreal. Bob's Sportsman came with a fairly new set of Atlas 6:50x16 whitewalls (the original tires would have been Firestones). These were bigger than the tires on a regular Ford (which had 6:00x16s) because of the extra weight of the wood. Soon after buying the car, Bob started working on the order desk at Goodyear Tire and Rubber Co. of Canada and decided he must have a spanking new set of whitewall tires for his new pride and joy. But Goodyear had just terminated its production of 6:50x16 whitewalls. Bob couldn't sleep at night, tormented at the thought of doing without a new set of whitewalls.

Then he hit upon the answer. He went to Vincent's Auto Wreckers in Ville St. Pierre (he had gone to school with the fellows who ran it) and spent all day Saturday searching through their pile of rims until he came up with five 1948 Merc fifteen-inch rims. Then Bob ordered five new 6:70x15 whitewalls through Goodyear, paying the dealer price minus the 25 percent employee discount.

But now the Sportsman beauty rings did not fit the fifteen-inch rims. Bob solved this problem when he acquired some snazzy-looking 1948 Chrysler wheel discs.

The factory-installed power windows on Bob's convertible (standard equipment on all 1946–48 Sportsmans) never worked properly, and he finally replaced all of them with crank-operated window regulators. He found one front regulator in Burlington, Vermont, on July 19, 1955 for $3.75. The other front one came from a Ford dealer in Ottawa, and two rears (used) came from Elliott's wrecking yard in Newtonville, Ontario (still in business today).

Before Bob made this change, the driver's window wouldn't stay up, and this became a serious problem when the winter of 1954–55 blew into Montreal. To keep the window up, Bob drilled a hole through the bottom of the chrome window frame, then inserted a bolt that rested on the window sill. Now Bob could keep warm while driving through the snow. Then one night, he pulled into the Orange Julep, a drive-in restaurant with carhop service on Decarie Boulevard across from the Blue Bonnet race track. When the tray of food arrived for Bob and his girlfriend, the carhop motioned for Bob to put his window down. Instead, Bob opened the door and began pulling the tray into the car.

Thinking he was trying to steal the tray, the carhop wouldn't let go of it — and Bob spent the better part of the next five minutes explaining why he couldn't put his window down. Finally convinced, the car hop let go and Bob closed his door. He and his date then proceeded to eat their food, which by now was cold.

In the summer of 1956, Bob and his brother Ed drove the '47 Sportsman to the Gaspe Peninsula to visit the town of Sayabec, where Bob and his two brothers had learned to speak fluent French. Meanwhile, Bob's friend Tony Myles was visiting his parents in Campbellton, New Brunswick. On the way back to Montreal from Sayabec, Bob and Ed spent a weekend with Tony and his parents. So far, on this trip, the '47 had been running just fine.

Finally it was time to return to the big city. The next day, Bob, Ed, and Tony pulled out of Campbellton at 6:00 a.m. for the long drive back to Montreal. Tony's mother had prepared a box of sandwiches and some cold drinks in a cooler to keep the boys nourished while on the road.

About four and a half hours later, disaster struck. The boys were approaching the tiny French-Canadian village of St. Fabien when the engine in Bob's '47 went Ping! Ping! Ping! — followed by a wrist pin ending up on the road. The engine had blown itself out, and Bob's wood-bodied convertible rolled to a stop at the side of the road.

But every dark cloud has a silver lining, and Bob's luck pulled him through. A White Rose gas station and repair garage was just across the road, and although it was closed for Sunday, the garage owner lived next door. He took Bob to the back of his shop and showed him a flathead V8 mounted on an engine stand. It had come out of a Ford pickup truck hit by a train a few weeks before.

What luck! Half an hour later, Bob, Ed, and Tony boarded the bus passing through town, which took them to Quebec City, then on to Montreal. A week later, Bob returned to St. Fabien to pick up his ragtop, now powered by a Ford truck engine. The engine with installation ("Motor posee") came to $85, plus hoses and water pump and tax for a total of $97.47. Bob purchased $2.53 worth of gas to bring the bill to an even $100. The truck clutch grabbed really well, and Bob drove away smiling.

On Saturday, April 24, 1954, exactly one month to the day from buying the car, Bob spent two dollars and seventy-four cents for some clips and fender moulding at Blue Bonnets Automobile at 7955-65 Decarie Boulevard. On that same day, he also went to Scarfe & Co. Ltd. to buy 1/4 gallon (#9771) Super Spar ($1.93), 1/4 gallon paint and varnish remover ($1.10), 1/8 gallon #1626 Red Maple oil stain (80 cents), 1/4 gallon alcohol (60 cents), and two sheets of #30 sandpaper (5 cents). Bob paid a total of $4.71 that day to preserve, protect, and glamorize the wood finish on his rare ragtop. But the cost of maintaining his wood-bodied convertible continued to climb. Bob returned to Scarfe & Co on May 22, 1954, to buy more sandpaper (thirty cents' worth). And over two years later, on August 18, 1956, Bob walked into the Canadian Tire store at 1465 Jean-Talon East to spend thirty-nine cents on a can of plastic wood. By this time, Bob had developed the habit of standing in front of the places where the wood had rotted away whenever he had his picture taken with the car.

To impress the girls, Bob's car had to make a lot of noise. On June 1, 1955, he stopped at Kendon's Fina service station at 5305 Cote de Liesse Road in the Montreal suburb of Lachine and purchased a dual exhaust kit for $36 plus 50 cents for pipe straightening and $2 for a pair of echo cans. Now Bob's car growled and rumbled like a moose at the height of the mating season.

He took his car to Hart Motors several times for servicing, which included tune-ups, brake work, a fuel pump gasket, a new low gear, electrical repairs, and so on. The receipts Bob saved provide a record of the mileage he accumulated on the car, since most of these receipts give the odometer reading. On June 30, 1954, the mileage stood at 69,576 miles (presumably original and the first time around). By September 18 of that year, he had pushed the mileage up to 71,900. By December 9, it read 73,560. By June 10, 1955, it read 77,700. On Saturday, May 19, 1956, it had reached 86,300. And on August 11, 1956, the Hart Motors receipt shows the mileage to be exactly 99,999!

In the fall of 1956, Bob visited Toronto and found a low-mileage 1950 Chev coupe. He bought it and sold his '47 Sportsman — still running — to Pat Cosgrove of Verdun, Quebec, for $200. Three years later, Bob and Pat worked together at Sept-Isles, and Pat made no mention of the '47. Presumably by then, he had sold it too.

Bob James

BOB JAMES FLASHES A "COCA-COLA" smile from the side of the road on a holiday trip to Maryland in the summer of 1955. The open passenger door shows the window crank installed by Bob to replace the cream-coloured plastic electric window button.

Bob James and his friend Bruce James (no relation) stopped overnight at this tourist home in Maryland. Motels were now becoming popular, and tourist homes for the most part faded into history until recent years, when their popularity surged as "bed and breakfasts." Bob's 1947 convertible is parked in the driveway. Note the 1955 Quebec license plate.

Bob James's 1947 Ford Sportsman was a far cry from his first vehicle, a pedal car with four-year-old Bob behind the wheel in front of the family home on Connaught Avenue in Montreal in 1938.

184

Jim Onions

1954 Meteor "Niagara" Convertible

JIM ONIONS OF BRACEBRIDGE, ONTARIO, wrote:

During the winter of 1954–55, there was a long strike of Ford workers which included the shutdown of the Ford plant at Oakville, Ont. After the strike was settled, although the 1955 Ford products had already been introduced, I spotted a brand new 1954 Meteor convertible at Evans Motors, a Mercury-Lincoln-Meteor dealer near Islington Ave. and Bloor St. W. in Etobicoke (now part of Toronto). The car still had a wrapper covering the tan coloured top and the hubcaps had not yet been

installed. It was a beautiful Bittersweet orange colour with a jet black dashboard, white steering wheel, and a combination of Bittersweet vinyl and black fabric covered seats.

I rushed home and told Dad and we returned to inspect it. I found it difficult to believe my ears when Dad said: "Let's buy it. " He was driving a 1952 Monarch 4-door at the time! We were told the car sat on the assembly line during the Ford strike, only partially built, and this car, along with several others, had to be finished before assembly of the 1955 models could begin. The Meteor had a standard shift transmission, and was fitted with 6.70 x 15 tires, and the Ford flathead V8 of 255 cubic inches. The interior trim was the same or similar to that fitted in Mercury convertibles, but the floor mats were rubber and the rear ashtrays were missing. Other 1954 Meteor convertibles I have inspected over the years were labelled Rideau, with all vinyl trim inside. They also had 7.10 x 15 tires and automatic transmission.

As you can see from the enclosed photo, Dad's car was labelled Niagara.

It was a very sad day when Dad traded this car in at Cruikshank Motors in Weston, Ont., to purchase a 1956 Mercury hardtop. I couldn't afford to buy the Meteor, of course, as I was making the princely sum of ten dollars a week at Parkinson's Cities Service gas station at Bloor and Prince Edward while attending Royal York Collegiate.

When Jim and I met for lunch, Jim speculated on how his dad's Meteor convertible became a Niagara instead of a Rideau. The Rideau was the top-of-the-line Meteor in 1954. If you wanted a convertible or two-door hardtop (some of which had a see-through front roof), they were available only in the Rideau series. The Meteor Niagara was the in-between series and was comparable to the '54 Ford Customline (the low-end Ford series was the Mainline and the upper-end series was the Crestline. Meteor's low-end series for 1954 had no name). When the assembly line began moving after the Ford strike, the '54 models partially built were hastily completed to hasten the arrival of the new '55s. Assembly line workers may have grabbed whatever trim pieces were handy, whether or not they were correct. It's easy to imagine a worker attaching the Niagara nameplate to Jim's dad's Meteor convertible if Rideau nameplates were not at hand.

It must have left the factory as a Meteor Niagara convertible because that's the way Jim's dad bought it from Evans Motors. It may have been the only Meteor Niagara convertible built.

Anonymous

Canada's Answer to James Dean, circa 1954

ONE OF THE MANY INTERESTING characters I met while growing up in Leamington, Ontario, was this James Dean look-alike, photographed just after the release of *Rebel Without a Cause*. This fellow is now in his mid-sixties, still lives in Leamington, and says, "I was a rebel back then, and I'm still a rebel."

James Dean, of course, is no longer with us. He was killed in a car accident in California in September 1955. But his legend lives on every September when '49 Mercs from all over North America converge on his home town of Fairmont, Indiana, for the annual James Dean Memorial Run.

The Canadian "James Dean" we see here is leaning against a car — but it's not a black and lowered '49 Merc. It's an even tougher car — his dad's 1947 Hudson four-door sedan, built like a tank and strong enough to smash its way through a bank vault door.

Norm Lightfoot and Friends

NORM LIGHTFOOT PURCHASED THIS DARK green 1947 Mercury 118 convertible in Weston, Ontario, in 1955, and drove it for two years before selling it in 1957. It had a radio, spotlights, fender skirts, and extra stainless trim on the lower rear of the front fenders. Norm drove this car north to Muskoka cottage country many times, and he is seen here relaxing with friends on the car in the summer of 1956.

Before selling it, he carved his name on the steering wheel. A couple of owners later, it was purchased by Duke Deadman, a young hot rodder in the east end of Toronto. Duke remembers seeing Norm Lightfoot's name on the steering wheel.

A couple of owners later still, the Merc was purchased by Tommy Henderson, a young hot rodder in the west end of Toronto. Tommy also remembers seeing Norm Lightfoot's name on the steering wheel.

Then Tommy sold the car in early 1959 for a family holiday in Ireland. When he returned to Toronto, he looked around for a good used car. He found a '47 Mercury convertible for sale on a gas station lot in Weston — not the dark green one he repainted maroon and then sold, but a silver-gray one with red between the fender strips.

Bruce Beatty

He slid behind the wheel and once again saw Norm Lightfoot's name on the steering wheel! Someone had changed the colour of the car while Tommy was vacationing in Ireland. He bought the car, then sold it a second time and never saw it again.

Maybe Norm Lightfoot's steering wheel will show up someday at a swap meet, and maybe the rest of the car will still be attached to it.

Three Fellows in a Nash Metropolitan

PHIL AND JOAN LEWIS OF Toronto owned this green Nash Metropolitan convertible in Toronto over forty years ago. Behind the wheel is a young Mike Filey, the Toronto historian who wrote the foreword for this book. With Mike in the car are his two younger brothers, Bob (in front) and Don. Every time they went for a ride, Mike and Bob told Don to keep low in the back seat (if he stood up, the car would slow down). This photo (looking south) was taken in front of the Filey home at 30 Elvina Gardens in north Toronto. Phil Lewis operated Redpath Pharmacy, and Mike still keeps in touch.

Built in England and shipped to North America beginning in 1954, these tiny two-passenger cars (available as a hardtop or con-vertible) sold well throughout the rest of the 1950s; the best year was 1959, with over twenty thousand sold. It was dropped in mid-1960, a victim of the new compact cars offered that year by the Big Three. Ford built the Falcon, Chrysler the Valiant, and GM the air-cooled, rear-engined Corvair. The Nash Metropolitan was well named — a good city car, especially for Metropolitan Toronto. At least one Nash Metropolitan was sold new in Newfoundland — and it's still there, all original with only twenty-six thousand miles. It's red and white and currently owned by Rose Noel.

1952 Pontiac Hardtop, 1955

KEITH ROBINSON OF MOUNT ALBERT, Ontario, wrote:

In March 1955 I traded my 1949 Morris Oxford on a yellow and black 1952 Pontiac Catalina Chieftain 2-door hardtop at Bruce MacDougall Motors in Port Credit.

When I went there the salesman showed me a 1952 Ford that I tried out. I stopped for a train at the Hwy 10 crossing and when I started to proceed the car stalled just as a train came from the other direction, so it was one time a stalled car was a godsend.

When I returned, another salesman said the Ford was sold so they showed me the Pontiac which I bought for $1495 less trade-in of $350. I then went to work for the Department of Highways, first in Stratford and then to Kingston where I drove the car on the job.

I had a problem with over-heating. First the water pump was replaced and then the rad. This didn't correct the problem and finally in Kingston I traded the car on a new 1955 Chev Bel Air. Before I took delivery of the Chev, more over-heating occurred and I took it to Simmonet

Keith Robinson

Pontiac Buick in Kingston. The mechanic said it was either a cracked head or blown head gasket. It turned out to be a head gasket and this seemed to correct the problem. However, I had already made the trade. Other than the over-heating problem, the Pontiac was a very nice car to drive. It had a nice style and I consider it one of the best cars I have owned.

Ray McKenney

The front view of the '49 Pontiac shows Ray's wife, Dorothy, with three of their seven children. Note the sun visor and the famous Pontiac streaks along the hood, first introduced on Pontiacs in 1935 by a young car stylist named Virgil Exner. He later moved to Chrysler and designed the "Forward Look," beginning with the 1955 models.

The second photo reveals some restyling by the creative use of a two-tone paint job. The angle on the roofline between the two colours simulates the design of the rear window on Pontiac two-door hardtops of the early 1950s. Look closely at Keith Robinson's '52 Pontiac hardtop on the previous page.

1949 Pontiac in 1956

THESE TWO PHOTOS ARRIVED IN the mail from Alvin Shier of Calgary, Alberta. Alvin is a regular contributor to *Old Autos*, and since 1995 he has been compiling a Canadian Pontiac Registry to track down and record the "auto-biography" (from owner to owner) of every Pontiac built in Canada since 1926. So far, he has collected information on over five hundred Canadian-built Pontiacs.

The 1949 Pontiac shown here was photographed in Ontario in 1956, when it was owned by Ray McKenney of London, Ontario. Ray recently sent these two photos to Alvin Shier to add to the Canadian Pontiac Registry.

1949 DeSoto from Alberta

JACK POTTER'S UNCLE WALTER OWNED this 1949 DeSoto coupe in the Peace River Valley of Alberta. After driving it for several years, he gave it to Jack, and that's when this car came to Ruthven, Ontario. It was written off in an accident a few years later and towed to Quick's Auto Wreckers on the Albuna townline.

The conservative styling was dictated by Chrysler president K.T. Keller, who insisted there be enough headroom for a man to drive the car without taking his hat off.

Bob Goodwin

1957 DeSoto Convertible, 1958

A FELLOW FROM TORONTO NAMED Gord owned this fire-breathing and tire-squealing 1957 DeSoto convertible, seen here at the drag strip near Cayuga, Ontario, in April 1958. The hood has been taken off to display the awesome concentration of horsepower between the two front fenders. The owner customized the car with imitation leopard upholstery, after-market fender skirts, and the removal of stainless side trim. Some 1957 DeSotos were sold with only two headlights in those U.S. states that had not yet legalized the new "quad" headlights. The DeSoto here has four headlights, a new trend beginning on only some new cars in 1957.

Walter P. Chrysler introduced the DeSoto in mid-1928 as a 1929 model, and it was an immediate success. Falling sales by the end of the 1950s prompted Chrysler to discontinue the DeSoto. Its final model year was 1961.

Carol Jones

White Rose Gas Station, Blytheswood

BILL KREPS AND HIS FAMILY operated this White Rose service station in Blytheswood, Ontario, from the early 1950s to the 1970s. One day Bill Cowan pulled in for gas for his 1957 Plymouth Belvedere two-door hardtop. This was the first year for *really big* tailfins on the Plymouth. Bill Cowan may have bought his car new at Hyatt Motors, the Chrysler-Plymouth dealership in nearby Leamington. "Try it at Hyatt and you'll buy it." The space-age styling of all new 1957 cars from the Chrysler Corporation inspired a memorable slogan for the new Plymouth: "Suddenly it's 1960!" In other words, the other car companies won't build cars this streamlined for another three years.

Ven Hardie

B-A Service Station, Toronto Area, late 1950s

VEN HARDIE (STANDING BESIDE PUMPS) operated this B-A service station at Sheppard Avenue and Kennedy Road in Toronto in the late 1950s, when this photo was taken. Ven started his automotive career at Ontario Automobile at 1001 Bay Street in downtown Toronto in 1934. He repaired cars and sold cars new and used during his long and interesting career.

The 1958 Chevrolet Impala convertible at the pumps represents a significant model year in Chevy history. That's when a new top-of-the-line series (Impala) was added to the Chev lineup, knocking the Bel Air series from top spot. And 1958 was also the year when Chevy introduced its first big-block V-8 (348 cubic inches) as a companion engine to the very popular 283 V-8 (introduced in 1957 as a beefed-up 265, which first appeared with the '55 Chevy). That engine now became known as the small-block Chev V-8.

Bringing Home the Groceries, 1958

RON PICKFORD'S MOTHER BRINGS HOME the groceries in the winter of 1958 in the west end of Toronto in the family car, a Prefect. Built by Ford in England from 1939 to 1953, the Prefect was a popular economy car in Canada after the Second World War. Ron's family emigrated from England to Canada in 1953 and felt right at home behind the wheel of their English-built Ford car.

Hungry for Horsepower, 1959

RON PICKFORD (BORN IN 1938) was not happy with the sluggish acceleration of the family Prefect. He was soon driving a car of his own with enough horsepower to rip the asphalt right off the road.

It was a 1939 Hudson coupe, which Ron found in 1957 when he accompanied his dad to the house of a widow on Dufferin Street who was selling her late husband's photographic equipment. The car had been off the road since 1941, and Ron bought it for twen-ty-five dollars. After some tinkering, he got it running and drove it home with no plates and no insurance. In no time at all he repaint-ed his 1939 Hudson coupe Emerald Mist Metallic and replaced the tired old flathead in-line six with a '57 Thunderbird engine with three carburetors. But how did he learn to do all this?

When Ron and his family first settled in New Toronto from England in the early 1950s, he found it difficult to make friends at school. He spoke (naturally) with an English accent, and the other students called him "Limey."

But his father knew what to do: "Son, you start fixing up old cars and you'll make lots of friends." To help things along, Ron and his dad excavated the floor of their single-car garage to install a grease pit (which was illegal in that neighbourhood). As the earth began piling up in their backyard, the neighbours began asking questions. And again, Ron's dad knew what to do. He told them they were building a fallout shelter to protect themselves from a nuclear attack. Since this was at the height of the Cold War, the neighbours seemed satisfied with this explanation. Ron and his dad kept digging.

New Brunswick Memories

LINDSAY MCALISTER IS A RETIRED Ford dealer living in Burlington, Ontario. His father, Stewart McAlister, operated a Ford dealership dating back to at least the early 1930s in Jacquet River, New Brunswick (halfway between Campbellton and Bathurst).

When the 1932 Fords came on the market (first year for the new Ford flathead V-8), Stewart McAlister ordered five of them, and they arrived by rail in a boxcar. He didn't sell any for a full year, and only after Ford offered a rebate on its new cars did he finally get rid of them.

All through the 1930s, he took in Model Ts as trade-ins on newer cars — and his growing inventory of Ts finally required him to put up some two-storey buildings to house them all while he was trying to sell them. This was during wartime, and because of a shortage of steel, he used British Columbia firs as vertical supports to hold up the buildings. One day Mrs. McAlister was driving another T into storage when she hit the wrong pedal. The T slammed into a fir and knocked it over. The Model Ts parked above her came crashing down. Fortunately, she escaped unhurt (which is more than we can say for some of the cars).

Around 1940, Stewart began selling Fordson tractors, and he asked his son Lindsay to try to sell one to the father of his girl-friend. Her name was Myrtle McIntosh, and Lindsay later married her. In other words, he was trying to sell a tractor to his future father-in-law.

Myrtle's dad didn't bite right away. "If you can plough my field with your tractor," he said to Lindsay, "I'll consider buying it."

Then Dad went into town while Lindsay started ploughing. He dug furrows nice and deep coming down the hill, but going up wasn't as easy. He made these furrows much shallower — but they looked good from a distance.

Myrtle's father bought the tractor, then later grumbled about the shallow furrows — but he got over it. After all, why stir up trouble with your future son-in-law?

When he got older, Lindsay slid behind the wheel of a 1940 Mercury and drove to Toronto to seek his fortune. He sold cars for Dane Hill, a Chev-Olds dealer on Eglinton Avenue West near Bathurst. Later still, he operated his own Ford dealership in Burlington. Now retired, he and his son Doug supplied, via Kent Weale, the photos you see here. Doug and Kent are brothers-in-law. Doug is married to Leslie and Kent is married to Sydney, who is Leslie's sister. Kent, incidentally, drives a beautiful 1933 Packard convertible.

All Photos: Lindsay McAlister

HERE'S A GREAT PLACE TO have your picture taken — on the hood of a '34 Chev. That's Myrtle McIntosh (Lindsay's future wife) and her friend Lois McMinn.

By the time this photo was taken, the '34 Chev in the previous photo must have had a flat tire because the sidemount on the driver's side is missing. Joseph McIntosh (Myrtle's brother) and a friend, Barbara Winton, are standing beside the car. Joseph appears somewhat camera-shy. This and the previous photo were taken in Jacquet River, New Brunswick, in the 1930s. The Chev probably belonged to the McIntosh family.

This young woman, named Frances, was a high school friend from Dalhousie, New Brunswick. She is standing in front of a 1936 Ford with a defroster glass on the windshield. Note the 1937 New Brunswick license plate.

Lindsay McAlister smiles from behind the wheel of a late 1930s Ford, a car no doubt obtained from his dad's dealership in Jacquet River, New Brunswick. The McIntosh family apparently preferred GM cars (as the two photos of the '34 Chev suggest). Can Ford and GM be joined in holy matrimony? Apparently yes, for Lindsay McAlister and Myrtle McIntosh got married. They say love conquers all, even brand loyalty. And years later, when Lindsay and Myrtle lived in Toronto, Lindsay was selling for GM.

This photo was taken in Moncton, New Brunswick, probably during the Second World War (note absence of front plate on 1942 Plymouth). Miss Lou McIntosh is sitting on the front bumper. All 1942 models were rare. Civilian automobile production in Canada ended in February 1942, when factories began to concentrate fully on war production.

By the late 1950s, Lindsay was selling cars for Dane Hill, a Chev-Olds dealer on Eglinton Avenue west of Bathurst in Toronto. This sparkling new 1957 Chev Nomad is gift-wrapped in the showroom in the hope that someone will buy it as a Christmas present. The dealership wrapped many cars this way as a sales promotion.

Dane Hill Chev-Olds, 1959

If you were looking for a good used car in June 1959 (when this photo was taken), you had a generous selection to choose from, all the way from a 1952 Pontiac to a nearly new '59 Chev. Note the string of lights above the lot to lure customers in after sundown.

While employed at Dane Hill, Lindsay McAlister sold this flashy '52 Olds two-door hardtop to a Mr. Lee, who was in the food business. His two daughters are posing with the car.

1958 Chev in Parade

Lindsay's four-year-old son Doug was photographed behind the wheel of this new 1958 Chevrolet Impala convertible driven (but not by Doug) in a parade. The keys are in the ignition on the dash, but safely out of reach of little Doug. Surely he must be thinking, *If only I was bigger, I could turn the key and step on the gas.* Doug later worked for his dad at McAlister Motors, a Ford dealership in Burlington. This meant three generations of McAlisters sold Fords.

Ten-year Drop in Price to 1960

WHEN THIS AD APPEARED IN the *Leamington Post & News* on May 4, 1950, the asking price for the 1946 Ford Tudor was $1095. If you knew how to bargain, you might snap it up for a cool thousand.

But if you waited ten years, look at the money you could save. It was Wednesday, September 21, 1960, when fifteen-year-old Paul Calderone purchased a 1947 Ford coach (virtually identical to the '46) from Target Auto Wreckers at 230 Eastern Avenue in Toronto for sixty dollars. But Paul had only forty dollars. No problem. The fellows at Target sold the car to Paul "as is" and delivered it to his home, then removed all four tires and rims and took them back to the wrecking yard until Paul paid the twenty dollars owing. Each week, he dropped by and gave them five dollars — and they gave him one tire on a rim. He and a friend rolled it home along the sidewalk.

Leamington Post & News

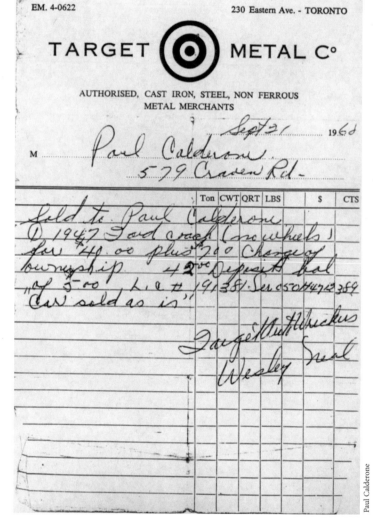

Paul Calderone

Paul Calderone

Finally the car was paid for, and Paul now had a set of wheels for bombing around town. He still had no license and no insurance. He was stopped by the police several times and fined ten dollars for driving without a license. He paid the fine and kept driving. When this photo was taken, he had managed to round up only one moon disc for the left front. The cigarette (Paul hasn't smoked in years) and black leather jacket blend well with the sixty-dollar car.

1931 Chrysler for $30

BILL WILLMS WAS BORN ON Friday, January 15, 1937, and grew up on a farm on the 5th Concession north of Leamington, Ontario, about two miles east of the old Leamington Side Road (now Highway 77).

Around 1957 he bought his first car: a black, all-original 1948 Mercury 114 coach for $150 from Murray Myles's used car lot on Talbot Street East in Leamington. The original owner might have been Frank Sherk (father of the author of this book).

In no time at all, Bill lowered the car, added fender skirts, shaved the hood and trunk lid, and replaced the original engine with a full-race flathead featuring three-ring domed pistons, a four-inch stroke, dual ignition, aluminum heads, and dual exhaust. Now he had enough horsepower to rip the asphalt right off the road.

With his foot to the floor, Bill stripped first gear so many times, he drove the car using only second and high. The engine idled at 30 miles per hour in second gear, and when he stomped on it at that speed, he could burn rubber right off the 8-inch slicks he was running on the rear. Then one day, the clip holding a wrist pin let go and it came right through the cylinder wall.

At this point the Merc was scrapped — except for the front fenders, hood, and grille. Those parts were given a new lease on life when they were grafted onto the front end of an old Chev pickup truck with front end damage. This Chevrolet truck was henceforth known as a "Mercolet" (*murk-o-lay*). Bill then purchased a 1956 Ford Fairlane two-door hardtop for everyday transportation.

But that car was too new. He wanted something older as well — and so, in the summer of 1958, Bill purchased a 1931 Chrysler CM-series six-cylinder sedan in Kitchener, Ontario, for $30. That was a whole week's pay back then. He spruced it up with whitewall tires and had his photo taken with it on the family farm north of town. He was working for the H.J. Heinz Company in Leamington at that time.

His '31 Chrysler was the fancy version of the CM series with dual sidemounts in the front fenders and a detachable trunk on a trunk rack at the back. Like other cars built in 1931, Bill's Chrysler had a fabric-insert roof. It was one of the first cars to have a grille in front of the radiator — and the '31 Chrysler grille was particularly stylish, mounted at a slightly rakish angle.

In sharp contract to the way he drove his '48 Merc, Bill resisted the temptation of driving his ancient Chrysler with the gas pedal rammed to the floor. Instead, he drove the car with the care and respect it deserved.

In the early 1970s, while still driving his Chrysler, Bill and his wife, Aggie, bought a farm on the 6th Concession north of town — and in the barn they found a new 1940 Ford bumper, still in its original wrapping! They advertised for anyone who could use it. A fellow drove up in a 1940 Ford and they gave it to him.

By October 1995, Bill's Chrysler was nearly sixty-five years old and he had been driving it for thirty-seven years. He took it to Carmen Paglione at Classic Collision near Leamington for some body work and new paint. He had already had the engine rebuilt and the interior redone. The following spring it was finished and back on the road with dark blue body, black fenders, and cream spoke wheels and pinstriping.

Bill Willms is still driving his '31 Chrysler around town. He's been behind the wheel now for forty-five years — and if you divide that number into the price he paid for the car, it works out to less than a dollar a year.

Ron Fawcett

Ron Fawcett with Two Model T Fords

Remember those Model T Fords you saw near the front of this book? We're now into the late 1950s, when the Model T began getting a new lease on life, thanks to antique car enthusiasts who started buying them and restoring them. Ron Fawcett of Whitby, Ontario, began rebuilding Model A Fords as early as 1942, and during the 1950s he scoured the countryside in search of Model Ts, which were by then in growing demand and going up in value.

Every time he found one in a barn, he trailered it home behind his White Rose gas station pick-up truck. He stopped at every station on the way home and put a gallon of gas into his truck (about thirty-nine cents' worth). A crowd would always gather to look at the T on the trailer. Then someone would say: "There's an old feller coupla miles from here with one o' these. Mebbee you ken buy that one too." For every hundred leads, Ron bought ten more cars. He's still restoring cars today in the large garage behind his home on Highway 12 north of Whitby. His restoration shop (Fawcett Motors

in Whitby) is now run by Ron's son, Peter Fawcett, and Art Carty.

In the first photo, Ron is bringing home an old Model T truck over forty-five years ago. In the second photo, Ron is demonstrating how you check the level of gas in a Model T gas tank, located under the front seat.

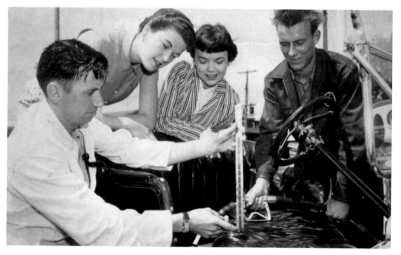

208

Customized 1960 Meteor Convertible at Autorama, Toronto, 1960

BEFORE THE 1960 CALENDAR YEAR had ended, the owner of this 1960 Meteor convertible had installed striped upholstery, lakes pipes, several extra tail lights across the back, and a shaved rear deck. The car was displayed on a carpet with autumn leaves at the 1960 Fort York Armoury Autorama in Toronto in October of that year.

Mike McGill

Mike McGill and the Etobi-Cams

AROUND MARCH 1957, A SMALL group of young hot rodders in the west end of Toronto formed the Etobi-Cams Rod and Kustom Club. By the time this photo was taken around 1960, club members had displayed their cars at shows in Toronto, London, Buffalo, Syracuse, and Pittsburgh. Front row: Doug Buchanan, Joe Calarco; middle: Peter Follett, Bill "Elvis" Foster, Ron Kearsley, Alex Weatherhead, Bob McJannett; back row: Doug O'Neill, Jimmy Brebner, Paul Fowler, Ken Gannett, and Mike McGill, who supplied the photos and the stories behind them. Their club name was derived from Etobicoke, the Metro Toronto borough in which they lived (now absorbed by the newly amalgamated City of Toronto).

The Etobi-Cams were affiliated with the local branch of the Optimists, a service club — and within a year and a half, these young hot rodders had earned the respect of the police by promoting safety on the road. Four of them had their pictures taken for the *Toronto Telegram* on Wednesday, November 12, 1958, along with Doug Buchanan's black "283" Canadian Pontiac-powered 1932 Ford five-window coupe. The Pontiac engine was installed under very unusual circumstances. Read on ...

Mike McGill

Unusual Engine Swap

THIS PHOTO WAS TAKEN IN Mike McGill's parents' driveway at 24 Leamington Avenue in the west end of Toronto. On the left is the tomato red 1951 Ford convertible Mike purchased from Barry Hallam right after seeing the car on display at the 1960 Speed Sport rod and custom car show at the Queen Elizabeth Building in Toronto. The bedroom window above the garage door played a pivotal role in an engine swap over forty years ago.

Back then, most teenage hot rodders were still living at home with their parents — and most parents were dead set against the idea of dropping a powerful late-model V-8 engine into an old car.

Doug Buchanan desperately wanted more horsepower under the hood of his '32 Ford, but an engine swap at home was out of the question, and having the swap performed at a shop (if you could find one daring enough to do it) was too expensive.

Mike McGill to the rescue! His parents were spending the sum-

mer of 1958 at the family cottage, and this meant Doug could perform his engine swap at the McGill family home at 24 Leamington Avenue. This street (a short one) is located less than a mile southwest of Bloor and Royal York Road. There was only one problem: the single-car attached garage at the McGill home had no overhead beam for the block-and-tackle required for the swap. The garage ceiling was a flat and smooth expanse of plaster and cement because Mike's bedroom was directly above it and none of the Etobi-Cams had a tripod for performing the swap in the driveway.

Then a brainstorm! The heaviest member of the club (Bob McJannett) was deputized to sit on Mike's bed in his bedroom. Under the bed was placed a large wooden beam extending out through the window and over the driveway. This makeshift "yard arm" was then fitted with a block and tackle and the entire engine swap was performed while Bob McJannett sat on Mike's bed.

Rust in Peace ...

NOT ALL OLD CARS GET sent to the crusher. Some are put out to pasture in wrecking yards across Canada, where they quietly disintegrate while being cannibalized for parts to keep other old cars on the road. This 1938 Dodge is slowly sinking into the ground at Elliott's Auto Parts on old Highway 2 east of Newtonville, Ontario.

Bob Kirk

Photo from Bob Kirk's Family Album

BOB KIRK OF WHITBY, ONTARIO, wrote:

This is a picture of my Dad and Mum beside Dad's newly acquired 1930 or 1931 Model A Ford, taken in Whitby, Ont., in the summer of 1945. Just out of the army, Jimmy Kirk married my Mum, Lillian, and bought this car, I'm not sure in what order. How much more could a man want? Dad had his girl, and his car too! And check out those two-toned shoes. Now the plan was to honeymoon to Niagara Falls.

They packed up the old Ford, including several spare tires, and off they went. Story tells it, although there have been many variations over the years, that they had about 15 flat tires. Yes, Jim and Lill got as far as Burlington and decided to turn back. They drove into Toronto, and had their honeymoon at the Royal York Hotel.

Later that year, the old Ford caught fire and burned up. He has had many cars over the years, and has always taken pride in whatever one he owned. In 1984 my Dad passed away, and my Mum is now in a nursing home, but what a memory we have because someone took the time to snap this picture.

Calling All Cars for Volume Two of *60 Years Behind the Wheel*

Do you have old photos of old cars in Canada (1900–1960) in your family photo album?

Would you like to see them published in Volume 2 of *60 Years Behind the Wheel*?

Please send clear laser copies and any background information to:

Bill Sherk
c/o *Old Autos*
348 Main St.,
Bothwell, Ont. NOP 1GO

Special Thanks

I WISH TO THANK MANY fine people for helping to make this book a reality. Toronto historian Mike Filey set the ball rolling by recommending me to Dundurn Press, where I met Tony Hawke, editor extraordinaire! Tony, Beth, Kirk, Andrea, Jennifer, Barry, and indeed the whole gang at Dundurn tackled the project with unbridled enthusiasm and carried this author on their shoulders all the way to the finish line. Any errors, flaws, weaknesses, shortcomings, defects, and examples of human frailty are mine. All mine.

I still don't own a computer, and don't even know how to use one (hence my nickname, "Dinosaur Bill"). Imagine my shock when Tony told me the manuscript for this, my fifth book, had to be delivered to Dundurn on a disc. A computer disc. I could feel the blood draining from my face. At sixty-one I'm too old, I muttered to myself, to be dragged into a high-tech twenty-first century.

Marg Baltzer to the rescue! Marg lives here in Leamington and is a computer whiz. She agreed to "disc-ify" my manuscript, and even contributed a computer-enhanced photo of her dad, Neil Quick, behind the wheel of his 1927 Model T Ford roadster.

Old photos of old cars are what this book is all about. Murray McEwan, my editor at *Old Autos* newspaper, very kindly loaned me many interesting photos from his files, and many fascinating stories along with them.

Other photos and stories have come from my own files accumulated during the twelve years I have been writing for *Old Autos* in my twice-monthly column, "Old Car Detective by Bill 'Sherlock' Sherk." To all of my readers who have contributed stories and photos to my column and to this book, I extend my sincere thanks.

Several of my fellow writers at *Old Autos* deserve special mention. My good friend Gord Hazlett is a national treasure and has already written three wonderfully nostalgic books of his own (*Old Auto Tales*, Volumes 1, 2, 3). Bill Vance has supplied valuable reference material through his "Reflections" column (syndicated across North America) and his three books (*Reflections on Automotive History*, Volumes. 1, 2, 3). Ed Janzen has contributed two of his wonderful "Manitoba Memories" and is currently the editor and publisher of *Canadian Stories*.

Jim Ervin has supplied a heart-warming story of his grandfather in the early days of Burnaby, B.C. Perry Zavitz has been a source of valuable reference with his all-Canadian book, *Monarch Meteor*. Jerry Petryshyn has shed new light on the history of the Russell automobile with his recent book, *Made Up to a Standard*. And Glenn Baechler has helped me in identifying the make and year of some of the oldest cars in this book.

Along with the late Hugh Durnford, Glenn co-authored *Cars of Canada*, the all-time definitive book on the history of all cars built in Canada. Published in 1973, it is still a monumental tribute to the fifteen years of research by its two authors. I consulted my copy almost every day while writing *60 Years Behind the Wheel*.

My good friend Alex Horen (who has two stories in this book) dropped by one day with a big box full of reference books on old cars. Thank you, Alex, for loaning them to me.

Additional thanks go to the members of the Leamington-Mersea Historical Society, the staff of the Leamington Public Library, the City of Toronto Archives, the Glenbow Archives in Calgary, Alberta, and the many other organizations and individuals who contributed to this book.

Special mention also goes to Jack Greswell of the *Leamington Post* for contributing some rare old photos from this area, and for helping me with the lyrics of "Mares eat oats…" Our good friend Robbie Marchand translated the back of a photo from French into English, thus adding another photo and story to this book. Jack and Harry Hartford helped me identify all five fellows sitting in a 1912 Model T in 1939.

My good friends Bill Myers and Bob Chapman assisted greatly in the story featuring Bob's 1931 Chrysler roadster.

And finally, special thanks to Mike Filey for writing the highly entertaining Foreword, and another special thanks to my good friend Bill "Wizard" Derbyshire for snapping the photo of me and my tomato red 1947 Mercury on the back cover of this book.

Bill Sherk,
Leamington, Ontario
August 5, 2003

Notes

1   Bill Sherk, *500 Years of New Words* (Toronto: Doubleday Canada Ltd., 1983), 200.

2   Glenn Baechler, letter to *Old Autos* (November 20, 1995)

3   Hugh Durnford and Glenn Baechler, *Cars of Canada*, (Toronto: McClelland and Stewart Limited 1973), 295.

4   Ian Marr, *Old Autos* (July 19, 1999)

5   Jim Ervin, *Old Autos* (February 17, 2003)

6   *Footpaths to Freeways* (Ontario Ministry of Transportation and Communication, 1984) 62–63.

7   Adrian Clements, *Old Autos* (May 4, 1992)

8   Ron Ploder, *Old Autos* (July 16, 2001)

9   Ed Janzen, *Old Autos* (Novenber 2, 1992)

10 Keith Thompson, *Old Autos* (February 18, 1991)

11 Gord Hazlett, *Old Autos* newspaper (May 4, 1998)

12 Marguerite Smith, *Old Autos* (Monday, August 7, 1995)

13 Ervin Groening, *Old Autos* (January 17, 1994)

14 Lloyd Brown, *Old Autos* (January 7, 1991)

15 Hazlett, *Old Autos* (May 4, 1998)

16 Sherk, *500 Years of New Words*, 248

17 Brock Silversides, *Old Autos* (March 21, 1994)

18 Hazlett, *Old Autos* (June 21, 1993)

19 Calder Hawkesford, *Old Autos* (December 21, 1992)

20 Janzen, *Old Autos* (February 21, 1994)